Nature Walks in Eastern Massachusetts

An AMC Country Walks Book

Michael Tougias

APPALACHIAN MOUNTAIN CLUB BOOKS
BOSTON, MASSACHUSETTS

On the cover: *Black Pond in Norwell, Massachusetts, see page 190.*

Maps: Victoria Sheridan
All photos by Michael Tougias unless otherwise indicated.
Book design: Carol Bast Tyler

Awaiting Library of Congress
Cataloging-in-Publication Data

Library of Congress Card Number 93-3988

The paper used in this publication meets the minimum requirements of the American National Standard for Information Sciences—Permanence of Paper for Printed Library Materials, ANSI Z39.48–1984.∞

**Due to changes in conditions,
use of the information in this book
is at the sole risk of the user.**

♻Printed on recycled paper.

Printed in the United States of America.

10 9 8 7 6 5 4 3   95 96 97

Contents

To my daughter Kristin,
who accompanied me on many a walk.
And to Fred Carty,
who knew the woods so well.

Acknowledgments

I'VE BEEN WRITING about special outdoor places in Massachusetts for a number of years now, and I often take them for granted. But every now and then, when I'm out in the woods, I stop and look around me and say to myself, "Thank God, somebody had the foresight to protect this beautiful place." Usually, I have no idea who that "somebody" was, but I'd like to acknowledge the men and women who, long ago, made the effort to save some open space for future generations. Today, more and more people are realizing the benefits of protecting wild places, and the work goes on.

A great number of individuals and organizations lent me a helping hand in the research for this book. The Trustees of Reservations, Appalachian Mountain Club, Massachusetts Audubon Society, Essex County Greenbelt Association, The Nature Conservancy, Sherborn Forest & Trail Association, Metropolitan District Commission, Massachusetts Department of Environmental Management, U.S. Fish & Wildlife Service, and a number of town conservation commissions all provided me with maps and helpful suggestions. I am especially grateful to Tom Foster and Wayne Mitton, regional supervisors for The Trustees of Reservations, who answered my many questions and shared their knowledge of the land and its wildlife.

A special thanks to Victoria Sheridan, who drew the maps, and to my editor, Gordon Hardy, whose knowledge and enthusiasm made this a better book.

Trail Key

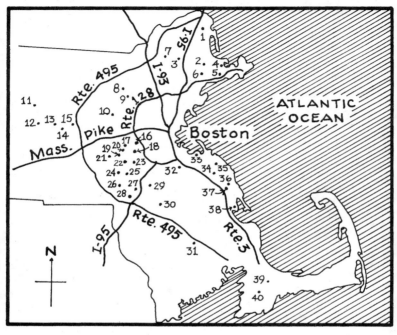

1. Old Town Hill
2. Willowdale Mill
3. Bald Hill Reservation
4. Stavros Reservation
5. Agassiz Rock
6. Appleton Farms
7. Weir Hill Reservation
8. Great Brook Farm
9. Great Meadows
10. Lincoln Conservation
11. Wachusett Meadow
12. Quinapoxet River
13. Wachusett Reservoir
14. Tower Hill
15. Gates Pond
16. Charles River
17. Elm Bank Reserv.
18. Noanet Woodlands
19. Peters Reservation
20. Broadmoor Wildlife
21. Rocky Narrows
22. Rocky Woods
23. Fork Factory Brook
24. Shattuck Reservation
25. Noon Hill
26. Stony Brook
27. Clark Town Forest
28. Hills State Forest
29. Moose Hill
30. Borderland State Park
31. Pratt Farm
32. Cranberry Pond
33. World's End
34. Norris Reservation
35. Black Pond
36. D. Webster Wildlife
37. North Hill
38. Bay Farm
39. Lowell Holly
40. Ashumet Holly

Introduction

WHILE EASTERN MASSACHUSETTS is home to a large urban area—Boston and its suburbs—there are a number of "pockets" of wilderness near the city where you can walk in solitude. Many of the locations described here are not well known and can give one the feeling of being in a remote area. Others are more popular, but they have "hidden" trails where few visitors bother to go. The reservations range in size from just thirty acres to well over a thousand. All of them are rich in wildlife.

For me, hiking combines the physical joy of walking with the thrill of seeing wildlife. A special day in the woods can make your spirits soar. Maybe it's during a walk on a crisp, colorful autumn day, or a winter's trek just after a heavy snow, or perhaps the first warm day of spring when all the earth seems to be awakening.

Of course, seeing a fox, coyote, or deer at close range can make any walk a special one. I've included some of my more memorable wildlife encounters in the book, such as the goshawk I saw at Bald Hill Reservation or the ruffed grouse that tried to draw me away from its chicks at Rocky Narrows. Just about every wild species that is found in the state can also be found at the reservations detailed here.

Each description includes directions, suggested trails, a map, potential wildlife to be seen, estimated hiking time, trail conditions, scenic views, and nearby points of interest where appropriate. We also mention if the trails are suitable for cross-country skiing, and if the reservation abuts a river, pond, or lake, the canoeing and the fishing possibilities are discussed.

I'm fond of quoting Thoreau because he spent much of his life exploring eastern Massachusetts, and he liked nothing better than a long tramp through the woods or a paddle up a river. He viewed walking as a way to lose oneself: "What business have I in the woods, if I am thinking of something out of the woods?" He walked often and far afield: "I think that I cannot preserve my health and spirits, unless I spend four hours a day at least—and it is commonly more than that—sauntering through the woods and over the hills and fields, absolutely free from all worldly engagements." And if Thoreau saw wildlife, all the better. It was not unusual for him to sit and wait patiently for some creature to appear, or stop his walk to watch wildlife for the rest of the day. I've found my own hikes to be infinitely more enjoyable if I follow Thoreau's examples.

My lifelong passion has been to explore Massachusetts, looking for off-the-beaten-path places. At first glance it would appear that this book and my prior two books are giving away my secrets and bringing more people to these secluded spots. But I've learned that people protect the things they love. I wrote this book to share some of my special places with you and hope that by raising appreciation for nature we can protect more wild places before they are forever lost to development.

Trail Courtesy

Respect for nature involves a few basic rules.

- Be sure to follow the "carry-in, carry-out" principle when it comes to trash.
- Do not remove any plants from the woods.
- Keep to the established trails.
- Give wildlife a wide berth. Binoculars and a tele-photo lens on your camera will allow you to view the wildlife without forcing it to flee.

By becoming involved in local conservation efforts, we can all help to keep our woods and waters in a clean, natural state, where wildlife has a chance to flourish. Besides local conservation commissions and watershed associations, there are also statewide organizations such as the Appalachian Mountain Club, The Trustees of Reservations, and Massachusetts Audubon Society, that have active conservation programs.

How to Use This Book

The walks are divided into five regional areas around Boston: north, northwest, west, southwest, and south. (If you are walking with children, see the recommended walks found later in this introduction.) Once you have selected the location you want to explore, and have read the property description, look up directions to the site under "Getting There" found at the end of each walk.

The approximate time it takes to make the recommended walk is given at the beginning of each entry. The time-to-mileage ratio I use is about thirty minutes for each mile, but if you're like me you will want to allow more time to enjoy the enviromnent. This ratio was used in some cases to figure approximate trail mileage.

You might want to take this book with you to use the map if you are unfamiliar with the property. A bold letter P designates the parking area found at the entrance to each site. Each map shows north to orient you, and we have included an approximate scale in either feet or miles. A heavy dashed line indicates the route described in the text, and the lighter dashed line indicates other trails in the area.

Conditions of trails do change from time to time and we would appreciate hearing about any changes you find. Address them to: Appalachian Mountain Club Books, 5 Joy Street, Boston, MA 02108.

A Few Suggestions

- To make your hikes more enjoyable bring binoculars, a camera, and a snack (food always tastes better in the outdoors).

- Unfortunately, it's not advisable for women to hike alone. Ask a friend who shares your love of the outdoors, or better yet, find a friend who spends more time in the malls than the woods, and introduce her or him to the joys of walking in the great outdoors.

- Getting lost in the woods is no fun. If you are unfamiliar with an area, be sure to allow plenty of time before dark when you set out. Even at the smaller reservations it's possible to get lost—I have. Always tell someone what reservations you plan to explore and what time you expect to be home. It's a good idea to carry water with you, even in the cold-weather months.

- The tiny deer ticks that can carry Lyme disease are spread throughout New England. Always wear long pants, preferably with the pants tucked beneath your socks. Avoid fields of tall grass during the warm-weather months. And to be on the safe side, give yourself a "tick check" after every hike by examining yourself all over, especially the scalp, neck, armpits, groin, and ankles.

- Be on the lookout for poison ivy—identified by its three shiny leaves. Again, long pants are recommended.

- During warm-weather months I carry a small backpack or fanny pack with water and bug spray.

- During cold-weather months I layer my clothes, taking my outer coat off as I heat up, but leaving on my hat.

- Deer-hunting season is in the fall, and I wear a blaze orange hat to be on the safe side—even when I'm in a no-hunting area.

Nature Walking with Children

A walk in the woods with a child can be a wonderful experience or a potential nightmare! The most important step you can take is simply to be flexible. High expectations can ruin any trip. Be ready to turn back anytime, and don't force your goals on a child. When a child shows signs of fatigue take a rest, then turn back—or you might find yourself carrying the child back to the car. And remember that walking in the snow, sand, or mud can use up twice as much energy as a walk of the same length on hard ground.

I've found that a little preparation goes a long way in ensuring that both adult and child have a good time. Bring a snack; oftentimes the child will be more interested in the snack than in the natural world. (There's nothing wrong with that; the idea here is to have fun and make the trip a pleasant one.) Bring a field guide to birds, animals, reptiles, and plants. A guide enables the child to work with you in identifying the natural world around him. Binoculars are always a big hit (there are some sturdy and inexpensive models for children), and if you do spot wildlife, binoculars might allow the child to see much more than a fleeting glimpse. Let the child hold the map, and have her help decide which way to go while you teach her how to interpret the map. You might also want to purchase the child a small backpack; from the child's viewpoint this seems to somehow make the trip more of an adventure, as if you are going to explore some far-off place.

Spending a day outdoors with a child is a great way to become closer and at the same time teach them a respect for nature. You can show him responsibility through your own actions, such as picking up trash—even if it's not yours. Try to see the world through her eyes and enjoy the simple things that feed her enthusiasm. (If the location has water, it's a good bet the child will want to spend some time throwing twigs or stones.) When you take a rest, that's a good time to tell stories about nature or browse through the field guide together. Remember to praise and encourage the child each time he learns something new or completes a walk.

I've found some of my best walks have occurred when I "let go" and share in the sense of wonder and discovery with my two children.

Recommended Walks with Younger Children

On many of these walks you should not attempt to do the whole route described in the book but rather a small portion, depending on the age and interest of the child. (I've labeled, where appropriate, partial walks, if the children are under six years old.) Generally, the walks listed here have fairly level terrain and well-maintained trails.

North of Boston:
Willowdale Mill
James N. and Mary F. Stavros Reservation

Northwest of Boston:
Great Brook Farm (to the pond area and back)
Great Meadows National Wildlife Refuge
Wachusett Meadow Wildlife Sanctuary (Swamp
   Nature Trail)
Tower Hill Botanic Garden (partway)
Gates Pond (partway)

West of Boston:
Elm Bank Reservation (partway)
Noanet Woodlands (to the mill site and back)
Broadmoor Wildlife Sanctuary (partway)
Rocky Woods Reservation (Hemlock Knoll Nature
    Trail)

Southwest of Boston:
Stony Brook Nature Center & Wildlife Sanctuary
Harold B. Clark Town Forest (for kids six and up)
F. Gilbert Hills State Forest (Blue Triangle Loop Trail
    for children over six)
Moose Hill Wildlife Sanctuary (Western Section; to
    the cistern and back)

South of Boston:
World's End (partway)
Albert F. Norris Reservation
Black Pond Nature Preserve
Daniel Webster Wildlife Sanctuary
Bay Farm Conservation Area
Ashumet Holly Reservation and Wildlife Sanctuary
    (to the pond and back)

Wildlife Watching

THE RESERVATIONS, sanctuaries, and conservation lands reviewed in this book are all rich in wildlife. Seeing that wildlife, however, depends on both luck and one's knowledge of the creatures themselves. We can't do much about luck, but there are a number of steps that can be taken to increase your odds of spotting the birds, animals, and reptiles that live in eastern Massachusetts.

Thoreau was an expert "wildlife watcher," patient and full of curiosity. He would think nothing of sitting for an hour to watch a bird or animal gather food. "True men of science," he wrote, "will know nature better by his finer organizations; he will smell, taste, see, hear, feel, better than other men. His will be a deeper and finer experience." I have certainly found that nature reveals more of her subtleties when I focus all my senses into the natural surroundings. Try following Thoreau's example and let yourself become absorbed by the forests, fields, and water—even if you don't see wildlife, the walks themselves are more rewarding and refreshing.

Two of the key components of wildlife watching are knowing where and when to look. The best time

to see most wildlife is at dawn or dusk. Many creatures are nocturnal, and there is also some overlap at
dawn and dusk with the daytime birds and animals.
Spring and fall are the two best seasons, especially
for migratory birds. Animals that hibernate will be
active during the spring after a long winter, and in
the fall they will eat as much as possible in preparation for the cold months to come. Winter has the least
activity but it does offer some advantages, such as
easier long-range viewing (no foliage) and the potential to see some animals crossing the ice (such as coyotes); also, animals are often easier to spot against a
background of white snow.

When people ask me where to look, I say "every-
where": in the fields, on the forest floor, on the water
or ice, along shorelines, in trees, and in the sky. But if
I had to pick the most productive single spot for seeing wildlife, I'd say it's the edge of fields. Hawks and
owls often perch here, and many animals make their
dens and burrows where the woods meet the meadows. Creatures feel safer around the edges—deer
often stay close to these fringe areas before entering a
field at nightfall. Red foxes and coyotes hunt the
edges, and they can sometimes be seen trotting
through tall grass on their rounds.

Another productive area is along riverbanks and
shorelines. Minks, weasels, muskrats, and raccoons,
just to mention a few, are commonly observed foraging next to water. And of course shore birds, wading
birds, and ducks are found here. Scanning a shoreline
with a pair of binoculars can be extremely rewarding—during a visit to a lake early one morning I once

saw an owl, a heron, and an osprey all within five minutes. Many of the wild areas in this book offer excellent canoeing, and this too affords opportunities for nature study at close range.

Obviously, when walking through the woods you must do so quietly if you hope to get near wildlife, but being quiet is not enough. Most creatures would

Patience and quiet, careful observation will reward you with the opportunity to see wildlife.

prefer to hide than run, and they will sit tight and let you walk right by. You should give the surrounding areas more than a casual glance. For example, when trying to spot deer I look for parts of the animal between the trees rather than for the entire body. I look for the horizontal lines of the deer's back contrasting with the vertical trees. Knowing the size of the animal also helps; when scanning for deer most people would do so at eye level, yet deer are only about three feet high at the shoulder.

Many animals blend in with their surroundings so well it's almost impossible to see them. The American bittern, for example, sometimes hides by freezing with its head in an upright position to match tall reeds and vegetation around it. A snapping turtle in shallow water looks just like a rock, and ruffed grouse can be indistinguishable from the fallen leaves on the forest floor. Even great blue herons will stop feeding and wait, silent and unmoving until perceived danger passes.

Another key factor to consider is wind direction, which can carry your scent to wildlife. If I'm traveling down a trail and the wind is coming from my left, I tend to look more in that direction since my scent is not being carried there. And if I have a choice when beginning my hike, I always travel into the wind. The same holds true when approaching a known feeding area. Serious wildlife photographers even go as far as wearing rubber boots to stop the scent from their feet from escaping into the air!

It is important, by the way, that humans do not approach too closely, or birds like the heron will take wing, thus expending valuable energy to avoid us. Many creatures will allow us to observe them, so long as we do not walk directly at them or linger too long.

Some animals are almost never seen because they are nocturnal and secretive. But you don't have to see them to know that they are present. They leave clues. You will find the tracks of otter, heron, raccoon, and deer along the soft margin of a river or lake. Hiking after a snowfall can be especially rewarding as fresh tracks can easily be seen. Some astute trackers can also identify creatures by the droppings they leave behind. The burrows and dens of animals reveal where such animals as the fox and groundhog live. Owls disgorge pellets, which can identify their presence and what they have been feeding on. Look for them underneath large pine trees. Deer leave a number of signs: the trails they use between feeding and resting grounds and the scrapes and scars on saplings caused by a buck rubbing its antlers. Peeled bark can mean deer, mice, rabbit, or others, depending on the teeth marks, shape, and height of the marking.

The time and patience required to find and identify clues can be significant, but so too are the rewards. It is satisfying to solve the wildlife "puzzle," not only in learning of a species presence but also to deduce what its activities were. Children especially seem to enjoy this detective work.

Besides using your sense of sight, you should use your hearing to help in wildlife identification. Many of us have heard the hooting of an owl at night or the daytime drumming of the male ruffed grouse. It appears that more and more folks in the outer sub-

Look in snow or mud for animal tracks. This is the heart-shaped cloven hoof track of a white-tailed deer.

urbs will soon be hearing the wild and eerie yapping and howling of coyotes. Some animal sounds are quite surprising. Creatures you wouldn't expect to make a peep can be quite vocal at times. I've heard deer snort, porcupines scream, and woodchucks grunt and click their teeth.

Knowing the behavior of birds and animals can often explain their actions. For example, if a ruffed grouse pulls the "wounded wing act," you can be sure its chicks are near and it is trying to draw you away. The mother grouse makes a commotion, dragging its wing in a way sure to get your attention. After watch-

Clues to animal activity can be found in the food they eat and the markings they make. This branch has been chewed by a porcupine.

ing the mother's act, take a moment to scan the forest floor and you just might see the chicks (look, but don't touch, and be careful where you step).

Another example of behavior that's important to understand is the warnings certain creatures give if you get too close. A goshawk guarding its nest will give a warning of "kak, kak, kak"; don't go any closer, it may attack you. (Never get too close to nesting birds or chase or corner an animal. Oftentimes the best way to get a second look at an animal is to remain perfectly still. They may return out of curiosity.)

Nature study is all the more fascinating when you learn the habits of each wild animal: what it eats, where and when it feeds and rests, is it active in the winter or does it hibernate. Birds can be studied in a similar way, and of course migration patterns are crucial to understanding when and for how long certain birds are in our region. Reptiles, being cold-blooded, are only active in the warm-weather months. Their temperatures vary with that of the surrounding atmosphere, so they cannot survive freezing temperatures. The relatively few reptiles that live in Massachusetts must hibernate in holes or burrows below the frost line during winter. The best time to see some of them is in the late spring; for example, that's when the snapping turtle comes out of the water to lay its eggs on land.

For wildlife photography, you need a zoom lens and a tripod. High-quality shots are extremely difficult. It's hard enough just locating an animal or uncommon bird, but finding a clear shot for a picture can be quite frustrating. Patience is the key—that's why professional wildlife photographers often spend days in the woods working from a blind.

Finally, don't discount dumb luck. Much of the wildlife I've seen has been by accident, but I greatly increased my odds by repeat visits to favorite reservations. After tramping hundreds of miles, I think I've now seen just about every species that's in Massachusetts.

But there are still a couple creatures, like the bobcat, that have eluded me and will keep me walking for another few hundred miles, I'm sure.

The Bay Circuit Trail

IMAGINE BEING ABLE TO WALK in a country setting all the way from Plum Island on Boston's North Shore to Duxbury on the South Shore. Of course Boston blocks the direct coastal route, but one day you will be able to hike the Bay Circuit Trail, a long-envisioned "emerald necklace" arcing through Boston's outer suburbs between Routes 128 and 495. Many of the reservations in this book will have portions of their trails designated as part of the Bay Circuit and it will be possible to walk from one reservation to another in an arc of green.

It is hoped that by the year 2000 the dream of linking open spaces surrounding Boston will be a reality, thanks to the Bay Circuit Alliance, a nonprofit partnership of public and private organizations. Bay Circuit Alliance Chairman Alan French estimates the total trail length will be 160 miles. Although the trail is primarily through woods and fields, some sections follow scenic country roads, passing by many points of historical interest. Spurs branching off from the main trail will lead to more wild tracts of land or historic places. In fact, the northern stretch will have one section heading in a northeast direction to Plum

Island and a second section going directly to Crane Beach.

Much work still needs to be done, but public interest and support for the trail has been tremendous. Carl Demrow of the Appalachian Mountain Club has been busy helping to plan the trail. Demrow reports that as of 1992 there is a thirty-mile section of trail already dedicated and marked with white-painted blazes and Bay Circuit emblems. It starts at the footbridge crossing the Ipswich River that connects Bradley Palmer State Park with Willowdale State Forest (see section on Willowdale Mill for an outing along the river here). The trail then winds its way in a generally westward direction, passing through Ipswich, Rowley, Georgetown, Boxford, North Andover, and Andover, ending at the Merrimack River near the Tewksbury town line.

Each year a "Bay Circuit Trek" has been held to promote the trail. The public is invited to join the Trek and hike all or part of the proposed trail. Carl Demrow is the trek organizer, and those interested in learning more about the outing can call him at the AMC headquarters (617-523-0636).

The concept of walking in peace and solitude through so large a portion of highly developed eastern Massachusetts is an exciting one. In many respects it will allow the nature lover to go back in time to when the Native Americans followed footpaths from one tribal land to another or from inland hunting grounds to the coast. The idea also has the potential to galvanize the public into action that will protect more of our open spaces before it's too late.

The idea itself is not a new one. Charles W. Eliot II first envisioned a network of easily accessible trails through adjoining conservation land in 1929. But it wasn't until the last few years that the effort really got going, and more and more of the Bay Circuit emblems are starting to appear at reservations. This state has a number of long north-south-running trails: the Appalachian Trail in the Berkshires, the Robert Frost Trail in the Connecticut River valley, the Mid-State Trail in central Massachusetts; now it's up to us to carve out our own path of green here in eastern Massachusetts.

Eleven of the areas covered in this book are on or adjacent to the proposed Bay Circuit. They are:

Old Town Hill Reservation

Willowdale Mill*

Bald Hill Reservation*

Great Meadows National Wildlife Refuge

Lincoln Conservation Land (Mt. Misery)

Rocky Narrows

Henry L. Shattuck Reservation

Noon Hill Reservation

Moose Hill Wildlife Sanctuary

Borderland State Park

Bay Farm Conservation Area

* Willowdale Mill and Bald Hill Reservation have been formally dedicated as sections of the Bay Circuit, with appropriate signs and blazes.

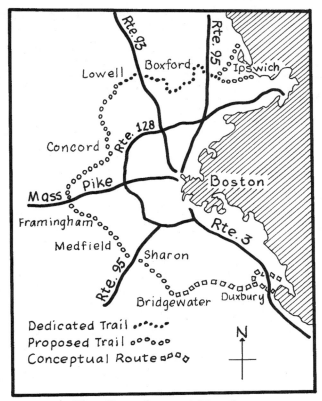

The Bay Circuit Trail

One complaint about some of the reservations in eastern Massachusetts is that they are too small. But with a viable Bay Circuit Trail, nature lovers will be able to extend their outings for miles. And now that walking is such a popular form of exercise, what better way to take a long ramble than to pass through meadows, marshes, and forest? Wouldn't it be wonderful if in the year 2000 we could realize the idea of a 160-mile-long emerald necklace around greater Boston?

North of Boston

Old Town Hill Reservation
Newbury
372 acres

Recommended walk: Loop of Old Town Hill,
1 1/2 miles, 45 minutes; Salt marsh walk:
3/4 mile, 20 minutes

Owned by The Trustees of Reservations, Old Town
Hill offers the nature lover a chance to walk to the
top of a wooded glacial drumlin and explore the
edge of a broad salt marsh. It's a very quiet area with
a good combination of coastal birds, inland birds,
and wild mammals.

Here's a hike where the road leading to the reservation is worth the trip in itself. Newman Road is a
New England country lane in the truest sense; farms,
fields, woodlands, pastures, and giant maples line
the east end of the road, making it a perfect place to
go for a stroll. Farther down Newman Street, to the
west, you will pass through a beautiful marshy area
that drains into the Parker River; it's a good place to
bring the binoculars and do some birding.

There are two entrances that lead to the top of
Old Town Hill, which means you can make a loop of

Only a twenty-five minute walk brings you to the summit of Old Town Hill. Here's a view of Plum Island and the Atlantic Ocean to the northeast.

the hill. I like to start my walk at the unmarked green gate on the right-hand (north) side of Newman Street. After reaching the summit, I continue to follow the main trail, exiting the reservation at a wooden gate also on Newman Street (see map). Old Town Hill is often less crowded than other nearby preserves: On a sunny March afternoon I counted thirty cars at the Parker River National Wildlife Refuge on

Plum Island and not a single one at Old Town Hill. My favorite season to visit this reservation is in the autumn when the hardwoods are ablaze and the trail, which is steep in spots, is dry. In the spring the trail can be a bit muddy but still passable.

Red pine, beech, oak, birch, and maple crowd the edge of the trail. On the left is an open field that is a good area to spot white-tailed deer. The deer population is quite healthy on the North Shore; in fact, on Plum Island and Crane's Beach there have been instances of overpopulation and starvation in recent years. The eastern coyote, however, has established itself here, and it's my opinion that in the long term they should begin to thin the herd. The fact that coyotes do prey on deer is becoming a source of much

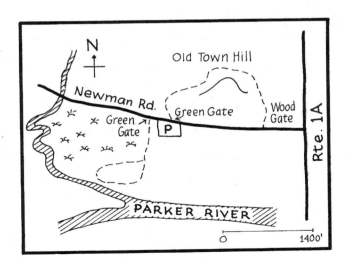

controversy, especially among hunters who feel the coyote may eventually decimate the deer herds.

Whenever you explore areas where deer density is high, be sure to protect yourself against deer ticks, the ticks that carry Lyme disease. Never wear short pants in the woods or fields, and pull your sock legs up over the bottom of your trousers. When you get home give yourself a "tick check," and be sure to see your doctor if you develop a rash (one of the early warning signs). I prefer hiking in such areas in the late fall and winter when you are less likely to be bothered by ticks.

It only takes about twenty-five minutes of steady walking to reach the summit. I would not call the views from the top spectacular, but they do provide good vistas of Plum Island to the east and Castle Hill and Hog Island to the south. The trail descending the summit is short but steep and will bring you back to Newman Street, where you can walk back to your car.

Old Town Hill has seen much activity over the years. It is said that the native Indians had a burying ground near the hilltop. Later, the first settlers cleared much of the hill for their sheep and cattle. In 1639 a watch house or sentry box was erected on the summit. It seems people were always erecting things on the hilltop; in 1926 a large redwood cross was placed on the hill and a tradition of Easter sunrise services began there. During a service in 1930 a church organ was even brought to the hill by a truck! Today the hilltop makes a quiet place to rest after a country walk.

There is a lesser-known trail on the other side of Newman Street (south side) that's something of a secret. Look for a green-colored gate just before Newman Street starts heading toward the marshes. The green gate marks the beginning of this wide trail. It leads to the banks of the Little River and Parker River (the Little River offers good canoeing through the marsh). This trail, with its open marshlands, makes a nice contrast to the wooded walk to the top of Old Town Hill. This walk only takes about twenty minutes. Be on the lookout for cottontails hiding beneath the cedars or sunning themselves by the edges of the salt marsh. Their brown coloring makes them difficult to distinguish against the salt hay and vegetation, but with snow on the ground it's much easier.

Getting There

From Route 128, take Exit 20 north onto Route 1A. Drive for 16.2 miles on Route 1A, then turn left on Newman Road and drive 150 yards to the entrance on the right. Park on the roadside.

Willowdale Mill
Hamilton
25 acres

Recommended walk: 1 1/2 miles,
45 minutes

Adjacent to the sprawling grounds of Bradley W.
Palmer State Park lies the smaller, lesser-known trails
of Willowdale Mill, a property of the Essex County
Greenbelt Association. Once the site of a nineteenth-
century textile mill, the land has reverted back to forest
and offers the nature lover a pleasant walk along the
banks of the Ipswich River. Wood ducks, screech owls,
kingfishers, downy woodpeckers, cedar waxwings,
and a variety of other birds can be observed here.

Begin your outing by following the trail that
angles toward the river (a northwest direction). A
large cellar hole and other signs of the old textile factory are clearly visible. The mill, which was located
just downstream of the parking area, produced
woolen goods such as blankets until 1884, when it
was destroyed by fire. You can still see the wide path
of the old sluiceway that channeled water from the
Ipswich River into the mill to provide the necessary
power. The trail follows the top of an earthen dike
that separated the sluiceway from the river.

About five minutes into the walk you reach the
Willowdale Dam. A small fish ladder carries both

The riverside trail at Willowdale Mill offers you a chance to see and hear the Ipswich River flow by. The trail is also used by wildlife as a travel corridor along the river.

anadromous fish (such as herring, which migrate from the sea to fresh water to spawn) and catadromous fish (such as eels, which travel from the river to the ocean to breed). Sit for a moment and relax to the sound of the falling water—it is hard to imagine that a bustling factory once stood nearby. I'm told the fishing can be productive for such species as largemouth bass; pickerel; bullhead; and brown, brook, and rainbow trout. On the other side of the river is

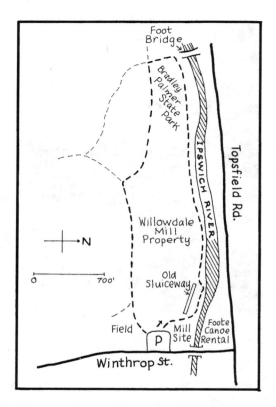

Foote Brothers Canoe Rental, something to keep in mind if you wish to explore the river by paddle power rather than on foot.

After passing the dam, the trail follows the river upstream through a pine grove. The pine needles carpet the path as the trail begins to climb a small hill. Oaks and hemlocks mix with the pines to block out the sun and the trail takes on a dark, mysterious look.

Be on the lookout for animals such as otter, skunk, and raccoon, all of which forage along the riverbank. I was once fishing along a river such as this, and had placed my catch behind me, when a raccoon boldly approached and stole the trout I was keeping for dinner. This "masked bandit" has a reputation for being fierce when cornered, so I swallowed my pride and let him take my fish. Watching him shuffle off into the woods, I had the distinct feeling he had done this before.

Raccoons are primarily nocturnal creatures so the best time to see one is in the late afternoon or evening when they begin to prowl about. They are quite at home along the banks of the Ipswich, searching for crayfish, turtle and bird eggs, frogs, grubs, and crickets. Baby raccoons are born in the spring and generally stay with the mother that first year, walking single file behind mom as they forage throughout the night. Many birdwatchers have mixed emotions about raccoons; while they are fascinating creatures to study and they play an important role in the natural world, they can wreak havoc on bird nests by stealing eggs. At my own home they have raided my bluebird boxes, and they always pay a visit to my garden just as the corn ripens.

As you continue following the river upstream, you eventually leave the Greenbelt property and enter Bradley W. Palmer State Park. I enjoy following the path all the way to the wooden footbridge that spans the river. Take a moment to walk out onto the bridge and watch the dark, lazy waters of the

Ipswich flow by. In the spring and summer you will be greeted by passing canoeists.

From the bridge, turn back to the same side of the river you were just on. Go straight as you get off the bridge a short distance to the next intersection. Turn left and stay on this trail as it hugs a small ridge line before it intersects with a wider trail, where you should turn left again. There is one more split in the trail, where you should also make a left just before you reach the field near where you parked your car. Without making any stops, the hike takes about forty-five minutes, but with the river-banks to explore you might spend a couple of hours poking about.

Getting There

From I-95 take Exit 50 to Route 1 north. Follow Route 1 approximately 4.1 miles and turn right on Ipswich Road (there will be a stoplight and sign for Ipswich). Follow Ipswich Road about 2.5 miles (Ipswich Road turns into Topsfield Road) and turn right onto Winthrop Street (just after Foote Brothers Canoe Rentals). Go a few feet on Winthrop Street, and just after you cross the river turn into the parking lot on your right.

From Ipswich Center, take Market Street over the railroad tracks. Market Street becomes Topsfield Road. Travel about 3.4 miles and turn left onto Winthrop Street (first left after LaSallette Shrine). Go a few feet on Winthrop Street, and just after you cross the river turn into the parking lot on your right.

Bald Hill Reservation

Boxford

(1,700 total protected acres in Boxford, Middleton, and North Andover
owned by the Massachusetts Division of Fisheries and Wildlife, Massachusetts Division of Forests and
Parks, and the Essex County
Greenbelt Association)

Recommended Walk: 3 1/2 miles, 1 1/2 hours

In central Essex County, sprawled over three towns,
are acres and acres of forested hills and low-lying
swamp protected as conservation land. The different
tracts of woods include John C. Phillips Wildlife
Sanctuary, Boxford State Forest, and Boxford Wood-
lots. The area encompassing Bald Hill and Crooked
Pond is generally known as Bald Hill Reservation. It
lies within the town of Boxford near the Middleton
and North Andover borders.

Because there are over 1,700 protected acres,
wildlife abounds; ruffed grouse, goshawks, barred
owls, woodcock, deer, fisher, and coyote all live here.
The uncommon pileated woodpecker has also been
seen here. It is one of the largest woodpeckers in
North America and can be identified by its red head
and loud, rasping call.

Wild turkeys have been successfully reestablished in Massachusetts, and these large birds are sometimes seen in the forest around Bald Hill. (Paul Rezendes photo)

Another large bird that inhabits these woods is the native American turkey. These birds are quite elusive, and in all my years of hiking I have yet to see one. But others have been more fortunate. Ed Becker, executive director of the Essex County Greenbelt Association, told me that one member of the Greenbelt had twenty turkeys cross his path while he was hiking at Bald Hill.

To begin your hike follow the main trail leading away from the parking area. (The trail has numbered markers at various trail intersections.) Overhead, hemlock trees shade this wide, well-maintained trail as it heads in a westerly direction. About five minutes into the walk you will pass a small swamp on

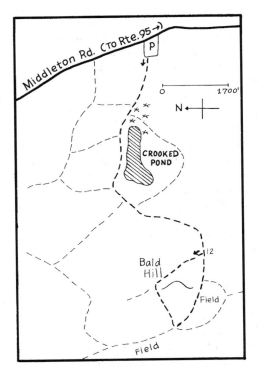

the left, followed by Crooked Pond, also on the left. There are a couple of openings to peer through the vegetation and scan this shallow pond's shoreline for great blue herons or visiting ducks.

Oaks, maples, and pines begin to join the hemlocks as you walk parallel to the pond. After you pass a trail that comes in from the right (at marker 13) the main trail begins a gradual climb toward Bald Hill. At marker 12, turn right to reach the summit in a short walk. Old stone walls indicate that this was once farmland, as so much of Massachusetts once was. The woods thin out farther up the hill and old apple trees can be seen among the small maples and oaks. There are no spectacular views, but an open field stretches along the ridge providing a nice sunny spot to picnic (which seems especially inviting in the autumn).

From the summit bear left where the trail goes downhill through the field. This leads to another open field where there are the remains of an old fireplace and chimney. On a recent spring trip I walked through this meadow and heard a high-sounding "auk, auk, auk." At first I thought it was a tree groaning in the wind, but then the loud noise came again and I started looking upward for a hawk. One more series of calls and I was able to pinpoint the source—at the top of a dead tree was a hawk with a long tail. It was a goshawk, a good-sized bird (about two feet high) with a grayish white chest. When the goshawk flew away it shrieked a series of rapid "kak, kak, kaks."

The goshawk is the largest member of the accipiter family of hawks, a rapid-flying hawk that feeds on birds and small mammals, including gray squirrels. They can negotiate their way through thick forest understory or fly just above the treetops. They are magnificent birds and rather uncommon. If you are ever fortunate enough to see one, you won't forget the way its red eyes stare at you—they can make anybody into an avid birdwatcher.

To begin heading back to the parking lot, bear left after passing the old chimney and walk in a southeasterly direction around the base of the hill. This brings you back to the main trail, at marker 12. After marker 12, more adventurous walkers might want to take a small path that makes a wide loop of Crooked Pond. The path is marked by a maroon dot on a tree and is between markers 12 and 13 (one map I've seen marks its beginning as 13A). The trail is rugged and hilly and adds about twenty minutes to your walk. I don't recommend it for young children because it's rough going.

The total time of this hike (without taking the Crooked Pond loop trail) is about one hour and fifteen minutes to an hour and a half.

Getting There

Take I-95 to Exit 51. Head toward Middleton (south) and take the first right on Middleton Road. Follow this approximately one and a half miles to a parking lot on the left, where there is a sign and a map welcoming you to Bald Hill.

James N. and Mary F. Stavros Reservation

Essex
73.5 acres

Recommended walk: $3/4$ mile, 20 minutes

The Stavros Reservation, a small preserve in Essex Township, includes one of the best lookout points in the area. The glacial drumlin called White's Hill rises only 116 feet above the Essex salt marshes, yet the views are absolutely spectacular. From the summit you can see Crane Beach, Castle Hill, Hog Island, and Castle Neck River. Although the property is small, nearby Island Road offers additional exploration. Wayne Mitton, regional supervisor for The Trustees of Reservations, notes that "Island Road is one of the best roads for birding on the North Shore." He's right; the marsh pools and fields attract all sorts of birds, so be sure to bring your binoculars.

The entrance to Stavros Reservation is on the right side of Island Road, just after you turn off Route 133. Park the car along the road adjacent to the welcoming sign and walk up the wide, wooded trail that leads gently uphill through sumac, cedar, cherry, and multiflora rose bushes. Within five minutes you see a vista of a rustic barn far below; a short walk brings you to the summit, where the views are even more far-reaching.

A sweeping view from atop the glacial drumlin known as White's Hill encompasses a salt marsh, the Atlantic, and Hog Island.

Once I visited on a warm October afternoon, when the autumn marsh grass was a golden brown, surrounded by sparkling blue water stretching out to the horizon. The panorama made me wish I was an artist—this would be a perfect place to set up an easel to try and capture the beauty below. Most folks

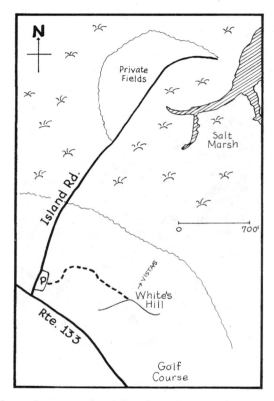

head north to see the fall colors, but a salt marsh in autumn is something everyone should see.

After absorbing the peace and tranquility of the reservation's hilltop, retrace your steps and take a stroll down Island Road. On my visit I saw two northern harriers (also called marsh hawks) wheeling, diving, and hovering just five or ten feet above the marsh. One of them swooped down and picked up something (probably a mouse or meadow vole) and then dropped it seconds later.

The marsh hawk can be identified by its long wings (forty-two inches from tip to tip), long straight tail, and white rump. They sometimes will make a sharp whistle or a call of "kee, kee, kee." It is the only representative of the harrier group of hawks in the United States. They are relentless hunters and won't give up easily on a prey, making repeated attempts to flush it out to where it can dive and snatch it in its talons. When courting, the male will perform incredible aerial acrobatics, soaring high then dropping into somersaults in midair. After mating, the female lays four to six eggs in a ground nest that both parents build. The nest is constructed of grasses and reeds, and it is used year after year, growing larger and larger with each new layer of vegetation. When the eggs hatch the nestlings are quite vulnerable to predators, so the parent hawks guard them closely, diving threateningly at any intruder that comes too close. These raptors are a marvel to behold, but, unfortunately, loss of habitat is reducing the population.

Other birds seen at Stavros include herons, kestrels, merlins, glossy ibises, egrets, and yellowlegs. A wide assortment of ducks can also be seen winging their way above the marsh.

Island Road is a narrow, dead-end street, best explored by foot. There are both cultivated fields and salt marsh along this quiet country lane. I brought my camera with me and must have taken twenty pictures—it seemed every few feet offered an interesting shot or new angles to capture the autumn colors.

Getting There

From Route 128, get off at Exit 14, then take Route 133 west five miles. Turn right on Island Road (immediately after Cape Ann Golf Course). The entrance to the Stavros Reservation is on the right.

Agassiz Rock
Manchester
104 acres

Recommended walk: 1 $\frac{1}{2}$ miles, 40 minutes

Louis Agassiz (1807–1873), professor of natural history at Harvard University, used Agassiz Rock to support his theory, which was controversial at the time, of glacial movement. This reservation provides an excellent example of how the great ice sheets of the ice ages shaped the terrain by grinding down mountains, carving valleys, and leaving huge boulders, like the two found by Agassiz, in their wake. Today you can view these boulders, known as glacial erratics (because of the haphazard way in which they were deposited), by taking a short, forty-minute walk around the property.

The trail leaves the parking area on the east side of School Street by the welcoming sign and first gently climbs the Beaverdam Hill, then later makes a rugged ascent to the summit. Along the way you will see many small boulders and exposed rock ledge lying beneath a forest of hemlock, beech, maple, pine, oak, and white birch. Mosses, ferns, and lichens grow well in these moist and shady woods.

It takes about ten or fifteen minutes to wind your way to the summit. (Stay on the main trail.) At the top of the hill lies the first large boulder, known as

When the glacier melted, this enormous boulder, called Little Agassiz, was left perched on top of Beaverdam Hill.

Little Agassiz. One end of the boulder rests upon a smaller rock. Little Agassiz is a variety of granite said to have originally come from the far north.

Take a few moments to examine the plants that grow on this exposed hilltop. Blueberries, bearberry (an evergreen shrub), and mosses give one the feeling of being on a mountain in northern New England. The vista from the top is primarily woods to the south and east.

From the hilltop, the path descends downward in a northeasterly then westerly direction. It is very difficult to find. First swing directly in front of the two hilltop boulders and look for the path just to the left of the boulders. (The path is quite narrow in places and it leads through a small swamp loaded with mosquitoes. Hikers with small children should avoid this path and descend the hill the same way they came up.) The trail winds its way downhill, and after about a ten-minute walk you will see the little swamp with the massive Big Agassiz boulder rising thirty feet upward from the soggy forest floor. No one really knows how many feet it extends below the swamp. Red maples, ferns, oaks, and hemlocks are scattered about the lowlands. Many hemlocks here on the reservation were killed in 1973 and 1974 by an insect called the hemlock looper.

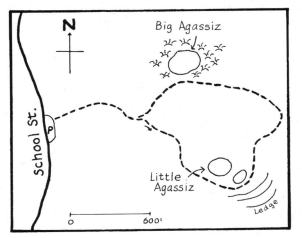

After a five-minute walk from Big Agassiz, the path intersects with the main trail where you turn right to head back toward the parking lot. Partridge can sometimes be seen here as well as an occasional red fox or the slow-moving porcupine.

The porcupine will den in hollow logs, deserted fox dens, or deep rock crevices such as those found at Agassiz Rock. I have even seen a porcupine make its den in an old culvert. When not in their dens they can often be seen resting high up in a tree, usually a hemlock or sugar maple. They feed primarily at night and will consume large quantities of tree bark as well as grasses, buds, twigs, roots and seeds. People have reported that porcupines have ruined wooden axe handles and paddles, attracted to the salt left on then by human sweat.

Porcupines are vulnerable to such predators as fishers and gray foxes. But the porcupine can inflict great pain by erecting its quills and quickly swinging its tail. If the tail comes in contact with the predator, the hollow quills expand as they absorb moisture. If imbedded deep enough, they can travel through the victim's flesh up to an inch a day. Sometimes a quill can even cause death. The old story that a porcupine can throw its quills is false. However, old quills do fall out of a moving tail and perhaps that is how the story started. Although quills serve as effective protection, the porcupine would prefer not to fight by staying in its tree or making a clumsy, waddling dash to its den.

Getting There

From Route 128 take Exit 15 and go north on School Street for 0.6 mile. A small parking area and a sign for Agassiz Rock are on the right.

Appleton Farms Grass Rides

Hamilton
228 acres

Recommended walk: 4 miles, 2–2 1/2 hours

Of all my walks described in this book, this one has the most confusing network of trails. But you shouldn't let that stop you from paying a visit to this reservation. It has good wildlife habitat, and the trails are so wide and the slopes so gentle it is a perfect place for cross-country skiing. However, it does seem as if a diabolical trail maker set out the trails with the intention of getting one lost.

After a few visits to the reservation and many attempts at mapping these trails, I called Wayne Mitton, regional supervisor for The Trustees of Reservations, who own this property. Wayne told me that the name "Grass Rides" came from the original use of the land as carriage roads. (The word "ride" comes from Europe to designate a path made for horseback riding.) Horse-drawn carriages would race here in the late 1800s and early 1900s, and that is why the main trails go in loops. Wayne furnished me with a copy of a map that I have expanded upon, and this should help newcomers enjoy the property without getting too confused.

The wide trails of Appleton Farms, passing through 228 acres of secluded woods, are excellent for walking and cross-country skiing.

The reservation offers a nice combination of fields, wetlands, and wooded areas comprised of pine, oak, maple, cedar, and my personal favorite, the dark-green majestic hemlock. I have seen a number of ruffed grouse here and many signs of deer. One animal I see almost every time I go is a fat woodchuck. They are fun to watch as long as they are not near my garden—after hibernating all winter, the woodchuck has a voracious appetite and will eat almost every kind of flower and vegetable, preferring the cold-weather crops, such as peas, to dine on first. When threatened they seek the safety of their burrows, which can extend underground for many yards and usually have two entrances.

Appleton Farms is believed to be the oldest farm in continuous operation in the United States. Its

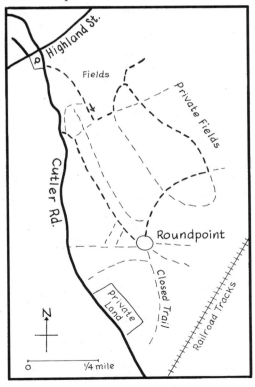

plantings back to 1638, when the town of Ipswich granted the land to Thomas Appleton. The descendants of the original owner gave some of the land to The Trustees of Reservations in 1970, and today it is open for all to enjoy (and perhaps get lost in as I have!). Please note that adjacent Appleton Farm is still private property and is not open to the public.

The hike I usually make is a circuit of the northern portion of the property. Start by following the signs from the parking lot that direct you onto a path that begins on the other side of Cutler Road and heads southeastward through a meadow. The trail soon enters the woods, and by taking the first left you reach the higher ground. At the next two intersections, bear left again. The trail soon follows the edge of the woods where it meets private fields. These edge areas are good places to catch a glimpse of wildlife such as fox or coyote that visit the fields in search of mice. While these predators are primarily nocturnal, they are often seen in the middle of the afternoon. I once saw a fox hunting at the edge of a field such as this at noontime; the fox saw me watching but didn't seem to mind as I was quite a distance away.

Retrace your steps a short distance back to the last intersection, which was located just before the trail curved toward the field. Follow this trail to the southeast, past one intersection that appears shortly, and go about $3/8$ of a mile to the second intersection, where you turn right. Notice the wide assortment of wildflowers, which include lady's slipper, Canada mayflower, starflower, violet, and wild indigo. (Saint-John's-wort, meadowsweet, bluets, and other wildflowers that thrive in clearings can be seen in the field near the parking area.)

About fifteen minutes down this trail you arrive at Roundpoint. This circular area is like the center of a wheel with spokes (trails) heading out in various directions. A strange granite pinnacle rests in the center of Roundpoint. This unlikely looking object was taken from Gore Hall, the former Harvard College Library. Francis Appleton was the chairman of Harvard's library committee at the time Gore Hall was torn down and he received this pinnacle, which was placed at Roundpoint in 1914, on his sixtieth birthday.

To return to the parking area, stand at the end of the trail you just walked down and face Roundpoint. The trail immediately to your right is the one you want to take. This will lead to Cutler Road after about a half-mile of walking. When you reach Cutler Road go right (north), and from there it is a short walk to your car. One word of advice: Allow yourself plenty of time before dark before you embark on this hike. The hike itself takes only about two or two and a half hours, but the maze of trails could get you temporarily lost.

Getting There

From Route 128 take Exit 20N. Go on Route 1A north for 4.5 miles. Take a left onto Cutler Road and go 2.2 miles to the intersection with Highland Street, where there is a parking area on the left. To enter the reservation, park and walk across Cutler Road and follow the sign and trail that are at the edge of the field opposite the parking area.

Weir Hill Reservation
North Andover
192 acres

Recommended walk: 2 1/2–3 miles, 1 1/2 hours

Weir Hill Reservation combines the best of woodlands, fields, and water. A hiker not only gets treated to views from the hilltop but also from the shores of beautiful Lake Cochichewick, a water-supply reservoir. The reservation got its name from the fish weirs that the Indians once constructed in nearby Cochichewick Brook. The weir (usually a woven fence) would trap migrating fish on their way to the lake.

Weir Hill is one of the few reservations where you can reach a scenic vista in just a ten-minute walk. From the parking area take the wide path, heading in a northeasterly direction, that leads to Stevens Trail and turn right. A slow and steady climb takes you beneath huge oaks. Within minutes you will enter an upland meadow with magnificent views to the west. The old mill smokestacks you see dotting the Merrimack Valley stand in sharp contrast to the isolation and greenery of the hilltop on which you stand. This hill is a drumlin, rising 300 feet above the surrounding countryside. Weir Hill, located a few hundred yards to the south, is roughly the same size, but the view is better from this meadow.

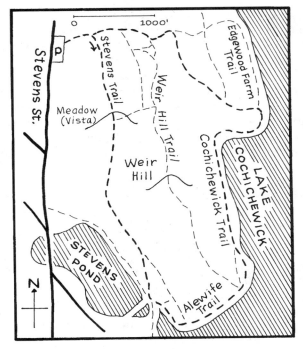

The meadow on this hilltop would be a fine place to watch the clouds sail by. At one time all the land around Weir Hill was open meadow to allow grazing for sheep and cattle. The early settlers of North Andover began clearing the virgin forests in the seventeenth century (the settler's axes and saws were busy throughout the state, and today there are only small, scattered stands of old-growth timber remaining).

It is possible to walk the perimeter of the reservation by continuing on Stevens Trail southward toward

Lake Cochichewick. I'd estimate that the entire loop is about a two-and-a-half- to three-mile walk. Autumn is the best time for this hike as it's more comfortable in the cooler weather without mosquitoes.

After leaving the meadow, continue on Stevens Trail as it heads down the south side of the drumlin. One of the more interesting features of the reservation is the difference in tree species between the east and west sides. The west side tends to be a bit warmer and drier from the sun while the east side stays cooler, with more moisture from the lake. You will notice that along the Stevens Trail are a combination of oak and pitch pine, while on the east side are maple, beech, aspen, white pine, white birch, and shagbark hickory. The fruit of these trees, especially the hickory and beech, provides food for a variety of animals that live on the reservation, such as ruffed grouse, oppossum, and raccoon.

Stevens Trail eventually brings you to a strip of land that separates Stevens Pond from Lake Cochichewick. There is an interesting stone arch bridge at this spot. (To stay on the Stevens Trail bear left, and do not cross the strip of land separating the bodies of water.)

As Stevens Trail passes Lake Cochichewick, the name of the trail changes to the Alewife Trail. It's a quiet, peaceful walk by the banks of the lake, made especially appealing in the spring when the shadbush blooms with white flowers. I visited here one May afternoon and had the pleasure of watching an eastern kingbird swoop above the water's surface catching flies. He then perched on a branch just

An old stone bridge lies by the shore of Stevens Pond and Lake Cochichewick ,at the southern end of the forest at Weir Hill Reservation.

above where I was sitting and preened himself, as if to show off after such an impressive aerial display. The eastern kingbird, a member of the flycatcher family, is best identified by the white band running along the end of its tail. Its head, back, and tail are black and its underside is white. They are known for their aggressiveness and will attack crows and hawks that venture too close.

The perimeter loop trail we are following along the edge of the lake changes names again after a short distance and is called Cochichewick Trail. The

Cochichewick Trail then intersects with a wider trail/dirt road where an old foundation can be seen on the shoreline. Go left, following this road as it angles back, gradually climbing up a hill away from the water. You will pass a impressive stand of large white birch on your right.

Stay left where the dirt road forks about 600 feet up. You will soon come to a scenic open meadow; landscape photographers will want to be sure to bring their cameras, especially in the fall. Just before the trail enters the open meadow, there is a small path on the left (Edgewood Farm Trail) that will take you back to your car, passing over a wooden footbridge and then beneath tall pines. Total walking time is about an hour and a half.

Getting There

From Route 495 take Route 114 east. Follow Route 114 into North Andover for about a mile, then take a left on Route 133 east and stay on this for roughly a mile. Turn right on Massachusetts Avenue. Pass the Common on the right, then turn left at the white church on Great Pond Road. After one block, turn left on Stevens Street. Continue 0.8 mile to Weir Hill entrance on right.

From I-93, get off at exit 41 and take Route 125 north 7.5 miles. Turn right at the lights on Andover Street. Follow Andover Street 0.6 mile. Bear right at the fork and drive 0.2 mile to Old North Andover Center. Go straight for 0.1 mile, then left on Stevens Street for 0.8 mile to entrance on the right.

Northwest of Boston

Great Brook Farm State Park
Carlisle
934 acres

Recommended walk: 3 miles, 1 1/2 hours

By keeping still, the great blue heron blended in perfectly with the rotting gray tree that stood at the edge of Meadow Pond. But it gave itself away when it snatched a fish, gripping it sideways, then working it around so it could swallow it head first. I got lucky when I spotted this heron, but how many others, I wondered, had I walked right by over the years?

The meadows, ponds, forests, and swamps of Great Brook Farm support a wide variety of wildlife for nature study. Purchased by the state in 1974, Great Brook Farm is rich in history as well as wildlife. The Native Americans planted corn and other crops in the fertile meadows here. In 1691 John Barett built one of the first cloth-fulling mills in America, later followed by a sawmill and a gristmill erected in the early 1700s. The power of the stream (Great Brook) was also put to work in the 1800s when mills made such items as wheels, nail kegs, and birch

A great blue heron slowly stalks the shoreline, looking for fish and frogs to snatch with its long pointed bill.

hoops. The mill site can still be seen at the northeastern end of the property just beyond where Great Brook passes under North Road.

Great Brook Farm has over ten miles of trails. The most remote paths lie at the southern end of the property near Tophet Swamp. My favorite hike, however, is a shorter ramble (about an hour to an hour and a half) around Meadow Pond. The trail is called Pine Point Loop, so named for its passage beneath towering white pines.

To begin this walk, exit the parking lot, go left on North Road, and proceed a short way where you see a sign at a beautiful meadow that directs you to the Pine Point Loop Trail on the right. Follow the path, bearing right as it brings you to Meadow Pond, a

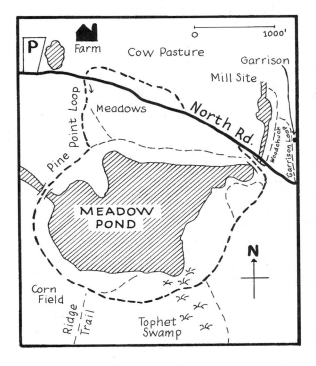

shallow body of water with different "fingers" stretching in various directions.

The trail is quite wide and flat, making it an excellent place for cross-country skiing. Picnic tables are scattered about the fields and woods, and one table looks like an especially good spot as it rests on a point of land jutting toward the water.

Stay on the main trail as it passes wetlands first, followed by a cornfield on the right. Listen for the screech of red-tailed hawks that often perch on tree limbs adjacent to the open cornfield. Various side trails on the left will bring you closer to the water if you wish to extend your exploration. The main trail soon passes through more low-lying wetlands, followed by a forest of hemlock, spruce, pine, oak, and a scattering of beech trees. Glacial erratics (boulders left over from the retreat of the last glacier) add diversity to the scene.

Just before the trail meets North Road there is a side path on the left that leads to a point of land topped with a large boulder at the shore of the pond. Bring your binoculars—it was here that I saw the heron. Another fascinating bird sometimes seen here is the wood duck. Nesting boxes have been erected on posts in the ponds to assist these colorful birds get reestablished in New England. The males are especially beautiful with iridescent greens, purples, and blues and a white chin patch. Females are a grayish brown color with a white eye ring. Their habitat includes wooded rivers, ponds, and swamps. They are fast flyers and are quite agile as they fly between trees.

Return back to the main trail and follow it to North Road where the waters of Great Brook tumble over a dam and out of the pond. If you follow the Woodchuck Trail across the road and along the stream it is only a five-minute walk to the site of the old mill on a tiny millpond. At the back end of the pond the water cascades over a waterfall lined with stones erected by the settlers—try to imagine the work that must have gone into its construction. The pattern of the lichen-covered rocks and the white water below make for an interesting scene.

As you retrace your steps toward North Road, notice a small sign for the "garrison," where the pioneers had erected a stone house for protection against the natives. If the approximately fifteen-foot cellar hole was the entire size of the house, it must have been quite cramped inside. Tight quarters, however, would have been the least of the settlers' worries during a terrifying raid.

Proceed back to North Road and follow that back toward the parking area to complete your loop. Along the way you will have the pleasure of seeing the farm and pastures on the right. Children will enjoy seeing the cows in the fields and the ducks in the pond near the barn. You can top off your trip with a visit to the ice-cream stand at the back side of the farm.

Getting There

From Route 128 take Exit 29 for Route 2 west. Follow 3.4 miles to the sign for Concord Center (Route 2 turns left here; you should go straight). The street you are on is Cambridge Turnpike. Follow this 1.7 miles to Concord Center. At Concord Center go straight to Lowell Road (Lowell Road is at the far end of the green). Follow Lowell Road for 5.7 miles to Carlisle Center. Go around the rotary and continue on Lowell Road for another 1.8 miles. Then turn right on North Road. Go 0.3 mile on North Road. Parking area is on the left.

From Route 495 take the "Route 2A East" exit and then follow Route 110 north to Route 225 east. At Carlisle Center go around the rotary and up Lowell Road for another 1.8 miles. Then turn right on North Road. Go 0.3 miles on North Road. Parking area is on the left after 0.3 mile.

Great Meadows National Wildlife Refuge
Concord/Sudbury/Wayland
3,000 acres

Recommended walk: 1 1/2 miles, 50 minutes

Great Meadows National Wildlife Refuge covers a large tract of wetlands abutting the Concord and Sudbury rivers. The diversity of habitat found here helps make this one of the best inland birding areas in Massachusetts. A total of 221 species of birds have been seen here in the past ten years. Great Meadows was first established in the 1940s when a Concord hunter named Samuel Hoar made the first gift of land. Today it is managed by the U.S Fish and Wildlife Service and has grown to over 3,000 acres.

The Dike Trail offers the best viewing by foot to see the wide assortment of birds that nest or stop here on migration. A small sampling of the bird life recorded includes great blue heron, green heron, great crested flycatcher, Canada geese, kestrel, bluebirds, osprey, northern goshawk, green-winged teal, black ducks, pintails, and herring gulls. On rare occasions, sightings of bald eagles and peregrine falcons occur. Binoculars can make your walk infinitely more enjoyable.

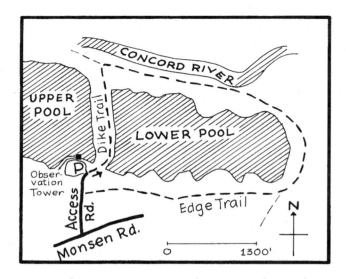

An observation tower, adjacent to the parking lot, affords a good vista of the wetlands. This walk will take us in a circular loop along the edge of the Lower Pool, which lies to the right of the Dike Trail that separates the Lower Pool from the Upper Pool. The Concord River lies just beyond view on the opposite side of the pools.

After enjoying the view from the tower, follow the trail that heads toward the open marsh (past the information boards). The wonderful swamp smells greet you as you follow the Dike Trail through the cattails that line the path. With water on either sides the Dike Trail offers the walker a feeling of openness. If you come in mid-August you will be treated to the peak blooming period of the American lotus, an aquatic plant with fragrant yellow flowers. Its bowl-shaped leaves are one to two feet wide and grow on stalks that sometimes rise over two feet above the water.

You are likely to see a great blue heron hunting the shallow water areas or perhaps perched atop the wood-duck houses that are scattered about the pools. One of the herons I saw was standing just a few feet from the trail; I got the impression it was used to humans walking by.

The mounds of dome-shaped matted vegetation reaching about three feet high are muskrat homes. Each house usually has one living chamber with one or more underwater entrances. Where there are muskrats, there are bound to be mink—look for them prowling the water's edges in the early morning. These sleek-bodied predators are excellent swimmers and their favorite prey is muskrat, but they will also take rabbits, mice, chipmunks, fish, snakes, frogs, and birds. On sunny days look for snakes sunning themselves on the edge of the trail. Benches have been placed along the path to allow you to quietly study the rich natural world around you. This would be a great place to watch the sun rise—which is also a prime time for seeing wildlife.

At the northwest end of the marsh, where the trail splits, follow it to the right. The Concord River lies to your left as you continue your walk around the Lower Pool. At one point the trail comes quite close to the river and you can follow a path to its banks. Thoreau preferred to call the river by its Indian name, "Musketahquid," which means "grassy banks." He spent countless days exploring the river and recorded the wildlife he saw, as well as the river's changing moods, in his journal and book *A Week On The Concord and Merrimack Rivers*. The river is slow and tranquil, perfect for canoeing with kids.

Follow the main trail around the back side of the Lower Pool and take the Edge Trail, a woodland path that hugs the edge of the wetlands. Pines, oaks, and maples are the predominant trees. Stay on this path and it will lead you back to the parking lot. The entire trail is about a mile and a half and is quite level, making it excellent for children. In the warm-weather months be sure to bring bug spray. Total walking time is a little less than an hour.

There is a short, lesser known trail in Wayland, called the Wood Duck Hollow Trail, where wood ducks are sometimes seen. It lies off Pelham Island Road, opposite Heard Pond.

Getting There

From Route 128 take Exit 29 to Route 2 west. Travel about 3.5 miles on Route 2 and then exit where the signs point toward Concord Center (this is at a stop-light where Route 2 makes a turn and you will go straight). You will now be on a road called the Cambridge Turnpike. Go 1.7 miles into Concord Center. From Concord Center take Route 62 eastward (right turn) and go 1.1 miles. Then turn left on Monsen Road and go 0.4 mile. Follow the signs to the parking area on the left.

Lincoln Conservation Land (Mt. Misery)

Lincoln

227 acres

Recommended walk: 3 miles, 1 1/2 hours

While the throngs of tourists circle Walden Pond in Concord, the woods along the Sudbury River, another haunt of Thoreau's, are relatively free of people. The town of Lincoln offers the hiker over sixty miles of trails in conservation land that encompasses approximately one-third of this quiet town. With so much land to explore, I've selected a trail system that is well marked and diverse in its scenery, wildlife, and terrain, around Mt. Misery. (Mt. Misery was so named, according to local lore, in the 1780s when two yoked oxen wandered there and wrapped themselves around a tree. Unable to escape, they perished on the hill.)

The Mt. Misery conservation land provides excellent views of the Sudbury River and Fairhaven Bay, while passing through a deeply shaded hemlock forest and a patch of open marsh. Wildlife flourishes along the river, and you just might catch a glimpse of a deer, barred owl, muskrat, or red fox. Two newer inhabitants, which also can be seen with a little luck, are the wily coyote and the beaver. The beaver has reestablished itself here (with help from the Mas-

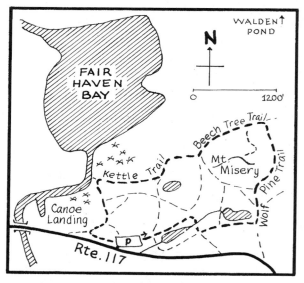

sachusetts Division of Fisheries and Wildlife) after being extirpated around the time of the Revolution by overtrapping and loss of habitat.

From his cabin at Walden Pond, Thoreau preferred to head toward the "south-southwest," which would take him along Fairhaven Bay and through the hilly region of Mt. Misery. In his essay "Walking" he wrote, "I can easily walk ten, fifteen, twenty, any number of miles, commencing at my own door, without going by any house, without crossing any road except where the fox and the mink do: first along by the river, and then the brook, and then the meadow and the woodside." He would walk every day and wonder how anyone could stay indoors. "I confess that I am astonished at the power of endurance, to say nothing of the moral insensibility of my neighbors who confine themselves to shops and offices the whole day for weeks and months, aye, and years almost together." Thoreau would probably be even more astonished by our society's development and commercialization of open space, but at least the acres around Mt. Misery have been saved.

A circular hike through the Mt. Misery property takes about an hour and a half, on gently sloped and well-groomed trails. The trail begins at a parking lot on Route 117. Enter the woods at the east end of the parking lot. The trails described here are part of the Yellow Disc Trails and are clearly marked by small discs. They circle the eastern end of the property, then loop westward toward the river.

Follow the path as it skirts the edge of a small pond then turn right, crossing a small stream that feeds the pond. Then turn left on Wolf Pine Trail, which passes another pond, and then left again, which brings you to the base of Mt. Misery. (The "mountain" is really a hill with an elevation of 284 feet.)

Stay to the right on Wolf Pine Trail to circle Mt. Misery as you head toward a gently sloping access road that leads to the summit. White-tailed deer are sometimes seen at dusk in the field on the right. The woods on the left are comprised of hemlock, oak, white pine, and an occasional white birch and beech. At the end of Wolf Pine Trail turn left on Beech Tree Trail. You will soon come to a fork in the trail; the path on the left climbs upward to Mt. Misery (only a partial westward view from the summit).

Continue on Beech Tree Trail. At the next intersection on Beech Tree Trail you will notice an old barrel wedged about fifty feet up in a tree. No, this is not the work of a flood! The barrel was placed there by the Lincoln Conservation Commission as a nesting cavity for barred owls. If you look closely during the spring and summer you just might see the fledglings in the nest. Be sure not to linger too long, as this might alarm the mother owl.

The barred owl is a relentless hunter, taking all sorts of prey, including mice, frogs, crayfish, insects,

The barred owl's large eyes, acute hearing, and silent flight aid its nocturnal hunting. (Paul Rezendes photo)

and small birds. The bird is silent in flight due to the soft edges around its wing feathers. That, coupled with its superb hearing, make a deadly nocturnal predator.

Conservation Director Joanne Carr told me a story about another bird of prey, the northern goshawk. It seems Joanne was walking in the woods when she heard a "kak, kak, kak." Looking upward, she saw the goshawk coming straight at her and she dove to the ground. The bird attacked three more times as Joanne retreated away from the thick undergrowth where the bird must have had its nest.

The goshawk is a relatively uncommon hawk that feeds on birds such as grouse and mammals such as squirrels. It is recognized by its long tail, short wings, and broad white eye stripe.

We continue the hike by following the yellow discs onto Kettle Trail (a right turn), which eventually leads to the edge of a broad marsh along the Sudbury River. The trail soon leads to the river itself, where good views are afforded to watch the waterfowl wing their way up and down the river.

Follow the yellow discs a short distance farther to complete your loop and return to the parking area.

Getting There

From Route 128 take Exit 26 onto Route 20 east. Go 0.2 mile on Route 20 and then turn left onto Route 117 west. Follow Route 117 for 6.9 miles to the Lincoln Conservation Land–Mt. Misery parking entrance on the right (just 0.7 mile after Route 117 passes the intersection with Route 126).

Wachusett Meadow Wildlife Sanctuary

Princeton
1031 acres

Recommended walks: Brown Hill,
1 ¹/₂–2 miles, 1 hour and 15 minutes;
Swamp Nature Trail: 1 ¹/₂ miles, 1 hour

At the center of Wachusett Meadow Wildlife Sanctuary is the old Crocker House on Goodnow Road. The house and barns are surrounded by aging pastures and acres of hay fields. On either side of the road, however, are two diverse forest tracts. Brown Hill lies on the north side; and with an elevation of 1,300 feet and an open summit it has an incredible view. To the south of Goodnow Road is a large swamp, complete with boardwalk, that offers the hiker a very different excursion. Both areas are home to a wide assortment of birds and animals that keep the nature lover coming back again and again.

Brown Hill Hike

By following the Summit Trail behind the Crocker House you can reach the top of Brown Hill in only twenty minutes. But don't go straight to the top. First, stop at a giant sugar maple that grows on the left-hand side of the meadow behind the Crocker

The giant Crocker maple, roughly 300 years old, graces the edge of the cleared fields below Brown Hill.

House. According to the sign nearby, the tree is "one of the largest sugar maples in the country. Its trunk is 15 feet, 5 inches in circumference and is 50 feet tall." The maple is probably 300 years old. One reason for its massive size is because it grew alone along the cleared fields with no competitors. It's a pleasure to

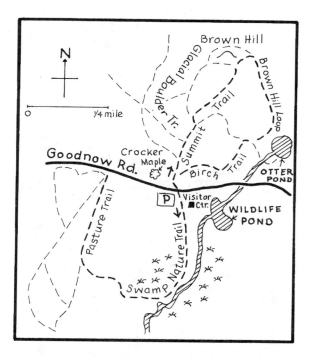

sit beneath this tree. I'm reminded of Thoreau: "Instead of calling on some scholar, I paid many a visit to a particular tree standing far away in the middle of some pasture."

Return across the meadow to the Summit Trail where you pass stone walls made by early settlers. It's a fairly short but vigorous hike to Brown Hill. Early morning hikers have occasionally seen a red fox or an eastern coyote crossing the trails. An even more unusual animal that lives there is the fisher, an active and wide-ranging member of the weasel family. The fisher is fast enough to bring down a number of fleet-footed animals such as hares, squirrels, and mice. It can even kill the slow but well-protected porcupine.

Fisher are long and sleek, weighing between five and twenty pounds, with males being larger than females. Their fur is usually a dark brown, except for their nose, legs, feet, and tail, which are a blackish coloring.

From the top of Brown Hill you can see a stunning, 360-degree view. Facing north and northeastward one can spot Mt. Monadnock in New Hampshire, as well as closer sites such as Wachusett Mountain and a near-by windmill farm. To the south lies Quinapoxet Reservoir and to the west is a picturesque view of a dairy farm. As you walk along the barren summit it's easy to feel as if you are in far northern New Hampshire. The cool, dry hilltop is reminiscent of a northern mountain, without the three-hour drive from Boston.

From Brown Hill I enjoy walking southeast down Brown Hill Loop Trail which passes through pines and oaks. A side trail (at marker 14) leads to a small meadow and Otter Pond, which is a small shallow pond where wood ducks, herons, red-spotted newts, and river otters live. At marker 12 turn left onto Birch Trail, which leads to the parking area. Exposed bedrock and gray birches are the feature of this path.

The total loop takes about one hour and fifteen minutes. On your next visit to Brown Hill try descending via the Glacial Boulder Trail, where an exceptionally large, rounded boulder lies. From the boulder it's a short walk down the Glacial Boulder

Trail to the Summit Trail, which leads back to the parking lot.

Swamp Nature Trail

I love this walk: Where else can you have easy strolling on a half-mile boardwalk through the heart of a red-maple swamp? The boardwalk allows you to enter the wetland and see closeup the swamp life that we normally miss: turtles, frogs, dragonflies, ferns, and sedges are scattered about the swamp. The five-foot royal fern grows here, giving one the feeling of being in the tropics. Some of the birds you may see include swamp sparrows, red-eyed vireos, tree swallows, gray catbirds, and several species of warblers.

The Swamp Nature Trail leads into the Pasture Trail (intersection post 7) at the western end of the property. Here I usually turn right, which leads back to the parking area, but there are still a number of trails to be explored by going left. The Pasture Trail passes through hemlock, beech, birch, oak, and of course fields and pastures. Before reaching the parking area the trail joins an old section of Goodnow Road, which is no longer open to vehicles. Notice the tall shagbark hickory trees that border the road. Massive stone walls line this peaceful old country road.

Getting There

From Princeton Center follow Route 62 west 0.7 of a mile and turn right on Goodnow Road. The sanctuary is one mile down. Admission fee, closed Mondays. All visitors must register. Hours are dawn to dusk.

Quinapoxet River Area
Holden
1,400 acres

Recommended walk: 1 1/2 miles, 1 hour

Located at the western end of Wachusett Reservoir, the Quinapoxet River Area offers hikers a bit of the north country in Massachusetts. A clear, cold, fast-flowing mountain river makes the Quinapoxet something really special in a region known for its dark, lazy rivers. The land around the lower portion of the "Quinnie" is owned by the Metropolitan District Commission and is kept in its natural state to protect this valuable watershed. For nature lovers this means towering forests, an abundance of wildlife, and a river clean enough to support native trout.

There are a great number of trails to explore, either from Laurel Street (on the north side of the river), or from River Street (on the south side). Laurel Street passes over the main feeder stream to the Quinapoxet, called Trout Brook. One trail follows the stream to the north and the other follows the stream to the south as it makes its way to the river. The area is a popular spring fishing spot, but come autumn the anglers thin out, leaving the riverbanks to the hikers. (Hiking, fishing, and cross-country skiing are the only activities allowed. This is a rugged walk,

A footpath along the edge of the swift-flowing Quinapoxet River. The river is known for its trout fishing, and the surrounding forest is home to deer, coyote, and fox.

with no formal trail system, so I don't recommend it for children.)

My favorite trail is the one off River Street that follows the Quinapoxet downstream. This trail begins at a bridge that spans the river about two miles up River Street from Thomas Street. The narrow trail begins at a steel gate on the far side of the bridge (north) on the right-hand side of the road. Walk straight past the gate a few feet and then follow the trail that angles to the right past the stonework of an old mill site. The path follows what appears to be an old sluiceway that is lined by a stone wall. About 300 yards down, the path arrives at the banks of the Quinapoxet.

The trail hugs the banks of the twisting river and the sound of rushing water accompanies you on your walk. Overhead tower huge white pines and beneath their canopy is a wide array of trees and plants: hemlock, mountain laurel, rhododendron, and dogwood.

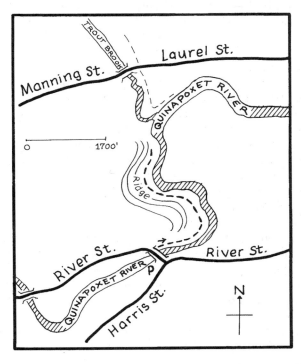

Growing low to the ground are fiddlehead ferns, lady's slippers, violets, lily of the valley, and other wildflowers. But it's the river that gives this place its charm; its rapids, tiny waterfalls, deep pools, and slow glides always keep me marveling at what a wondrous thing a river is. Native brook trout, holdover browns, and stocked rainbows call the Quinnie home. Almost all the upland animals live in the surrounding forests, and when I hike here I often hear the thumping, gaining in speed, of the ruffed grouse as it beats its wings.

About a quarter-mile downstream you will see granite blocks on each side of the river where an old bridge once spanned it. A wider trail shoots off to the north, or if you decide to stay along the river, a faint path goes through some rugged terrain before leveling out again. Sometimes the trail is inches from the water, other times it follows a ridge high above the river. I usually stop after thirty minutes of hiking, have a snack by the water, and then head back. (This is a large section of woods with unmarked trails and it's easy to get lost. I recommend staying on this river trail.)

The river is a popular fishing spot—this is one of the top trout streams to be found anywhere east of the Connecticut River. Trout fishing isn't nearly as difficult as the experts would have you believe: even fly-fishing can yield results for a beginner. Fish the deep slow pools or a patch of slower pocket water surrounded by fast water. Trout like to rest out of the main current in shady spots, such as behind a boulder or beneath the overhanging riverbank. Beginners should try spin-fishing first, using spinners such as

Mepps or Panther Martins. Always walk upstream so you don't spook these shy and elusive creatures. By walking and casting upstream the fish is less likely to see you or feel your vibrations. (Trout have their heads pointed into the current.)

A day hiking and fishing along the Quinnie is always pleasant, even in the rain (when the trout are more apt to strike). Remember to bring your camera to take a picture of your catch before releasing it to keep the Quinnie a productive fishery.

Getting There

From Route 495 take Exit 25 to Route 290 west. Go roughly 7.5 miles on Route 290 to Exit 23 for Route 140 north. Travel north on Route 140 for 7.2 miles. Turn left on Thomas Street (Route 140 curves toward the right and is called North Main at this junction with Thomas Street). Follow Thomas Street 0.4 mile and then turn right on River Street. Travel 2 miles down River Street. You will see where River Street turns sharply to the right at a bridge over the Quinapoxet River and Harris Street goes straight ahead. Park on the shoulder of the road on Harris Street or River Street. The entrance to the trail is on the other side of the bridge (north side of river) on the right.

Wachusett Reservoir, Reservation, and Watershed

Boylston/West Boylston
Approximately 8000 acres,
includes water surface and woods
surrounding reservoir
(Operated by the Metropolitan District Commission)

Recommended walk: There are a number of gates and access points to the forest surounding the reservoir. Two of my favorite entries are gate 10 and gate 14 at the end of Scar Hill Road. A walk by the Old Stone Church is also recommended.

Wachusett Reservoir was created in 1895 to solve the water needs of the greater Boston area. Today, the reservoir still supplies water to Boston (with the help of Quabbin Reservoir), but it also serves as an important wildlife reservation. Few people realize that the thousands of acres bordering Wachusett Reservoir offer tremendous hiking, cross-country skiing, snowshoeing, and wildlife watching.

Hiking is allowed in any area that is not posted. The entrances currently open are gates 6 to 16 along Route 70, gates 17 to 24 along Route 140, and gates 25 to 35 along Routes 12 and 110. The MDC is permitting

Loons are occasionally seen (and heard) on Wachusett Reservoir. They need large bodies of water for their takeoff into the air.

skiing and snowshoeing on portions of the eastern shore along Route 70 (gates 7 to 15) on a trial basis.

The deep, clear waters of Wachusett also offer the fisherman some tremendous angling opportunities for lake trout, brown trout, salmon, and some very large smallmouth bass. No boating is allowed, but shore fishermen can use the same gates open to hikers to reach the reservoir, or they can fish along the southern stretch where Route 140 parallels the shore. Wachusett has some special fishing regulations, the most important one being the limited season, from April (if the ice is out) to October.

The Wachusett shoreline can be walked for miles, and due to the size of this body of water, it attracts a

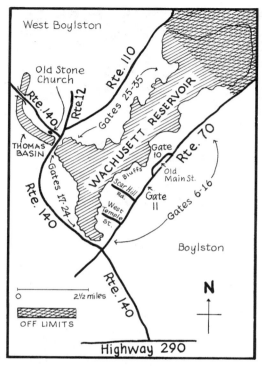

West Boylston

Old Stone Church

Rte. 110

Rte. 12

Rte. 140

THOMAS BASIN

Gates 25-35

WACHUSETT RESERVOIR

Gates 17-24

Gate 10

Rte. 70

Bluffs

Old Main St.

Scar Hill Rd.

Gate 11

West Temple St.

Gates 6-16

Rte. 140

Boylston

0   2½ miles

OFF LIMITS

N

Rte. 140

Highway 290

good deal of waterfowl, including an occasional loon. The common loon can be identified by its long pointed bill on a sleek black head with black- and white-markings on its back. If you are really lucky you might hear its cry, something you will never forget. The loon actually has a number of different cries: At night it tends to emit a mournful wail, while in the daytime you are more apt to hear its tremolo, which sounds like a demented laugh. Both can send shivers up your spine.

Watching a loon is absolutely fascinating, whether it is taking off, flying, or diving. It is a large bird, weighing about nine pounds, and it has difficulty getting in the air. That's why you never see loons on small bodies of water—it sometimes needs a quarter of a mile to flap its wings and run along the lake's surface to become airborne. But once in the air, the bird is quite at home, traveling at speeds in excess of sixty miles per hour. Equally impressive is the way loons can dive underwater in search of fish. They use their wings to propel themselves along underwater, and they usually stay beneath the surface for forty seconds, although they have been known to stay submerged for up to five minutes.

I once saw a loon at the southern end of the reservoir along Scar Hill Bluffs, a small cliff above the water. The bluffs can be reached by parking on Route 140 (just west of Route 70) and walking along the shoreline heading to the right. I usually walk about a mile and then take a long rest while gazing out at the water before retracing my steps back to my car. This section of Route 140 also offers good views of the reservoir and gives one an idea of just how large a body of water Wachusett really is.

Other good hiking spots are the trails that lead down to the water from gates 9, 10, and 14. (Gate 10 is my favorite.) Be sure to stay on the trails at all times, and remember the way you came in. You would not want to get lost in these sprawling acres. It is a good idea to travel with a friend and always tell someone where you plan to hike. Since there are no formal trails, first-time visitors and inexperienced hikers should stay near the shoreline of the reservoir. (The shoreline near the Old Stone Church is a good place for first-time visitors to explore.)

In various conversations I've had with the officials who oversee this watershed, they have told me they have seen coyotes, deer, and bobcats. They also do not rule out the possibility that a cougar might roam these woods. Every now and then there are reported cougar sightings in New England, one of the more recent ones being at Quabbin Reservoir in May of 1991. Surely these people are seeing something and it is possible that the animal was illegally released from captivity, or perhaps the cougar was never really extinct after all. It's fun to speculate, but until one is captured or a high-quality picture is taken along with clearly defined tracks, we can only wonder.

For history buffs, the place to go is the Old Stone Church, located on the shores of the reservoir just off Route 140 about 200 yards past where it splits from Route 12. (The street name for Route 140 along this section is Beaman Street, where the Thomas Basin section of the reservoir lies.) The stone exterior of the church is all that remains, as it had to be abandoned when the reservoir was created. Even though the interior has been stripped bare, it is still a beautiful structure to visit, and from this spot you can take a nice stroll around Thomas Basin. Large maples and pines line the shoreline path, and waterfowl can often be seen resting in the basin.

The Metropolitan District Commission carefully manages the lands surrounding the reservoir to protect the water quality and enhance the ecological integrity of this valuable natural resource.

Getting There

From Route 495 take Exit 25 to Route 290 west. Drive 7.5 miles on Route 290 to Exit 23 for Route 140 north. About 2 miles on Route 140 will bring you to the intersection of Route 70 at the southern end of the reservoir. From here you can go another 4 miles on Route 140 to the Old Stone Church or travel north on Route 70 to various gates. Gate 10 can be reached by driving 2 miles north on Route 70 and taking a left turn onto a narrow road (Old Main Street). Gate 10 is about 500 yards down on the left.

Miles of rugged forest surround sprawling Wachusett Reservoir.

Tower Hill Botanic Garden
Boylston
132 acres

Recommended walk: 1 ³/₄ miles, 50 minutes

The beautifully designed gardens and broad range of plants laid out by the Worcester County Horticultural Society at Tower Hill attract visitors from far and wide. There are over 350 species and varieties of trees and shrubs in the lawn garden to delight in and to admire, as well as perennials, annuals, and an orchard containing 119 pre-twentieth-century apple varieties. In addition to all this unique and colorful vegetation is a nature trail, often overlooked by visitors, that winds in and out of woodlands, meadows, exposed cliffs, and low-lying marshes. The diverse terrain allows for a wide variety of wildlife, and the staff at Tower Hill has constructed a wildlife garden to attract birds, bats, and butterflies (there are also plans to construct a rock garden and children's garden in the future).

When you arrive at the parking lot you will be rewarded by sweeping westward vistas that showcase the deep blue waters of Wachusett Reservoir and the distant outline of Mount Wachusett. Our walk takes us to the summit of Tower Hill (for an even better vista) and then circles the property's meadows and orchards. Benches have been strategically placed

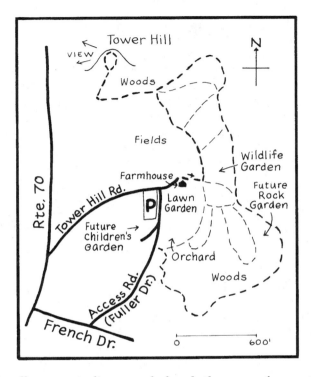

to allow one to linger and absorb the many fragrant scents, examine the vivid colors, and feel the tranquility and peacefulness of these quiet acres.

Begin your ramble by following the trail that leads east through the fields behind the farmhouse at the crest of the hill. (The construction area you see is for the Education and Visitors Center to be completed in the spring of 1994—trails here are subject to change.) At the first trail intersection turn left (north) and walk past the daffodils and wildflowers. Look for bluebirds hunting insects among the wildflowers. The bluebird is a social creature and males and females can often be seen together. Other birds seen here include swallows, wrens, titmice, finches, and flycatchers.

Where the trail approaches the woods turn left and follow it along the edge of the woods. The path soon enters the forest (a right turn, due north) and begins a gradual climb along a ridge to the top of Tower Hill. Stunted oaks and white pines do their best to grow on the rocky ledge. Two benches sit at the summit and the view of Mount Wachusett hasn't changed since Thoreau's days, when he described it as "the blue wall which bounded the western horizon." Take a moment to sit and enjoy the breeze and the panoramic view.

Follow the path back off the summit, turn left at the base of the hill, and walk along the edge of the field in an eastward direction. Look for hawks perched on tree limbs as they scan the field for signs of mice. Where field meets woods is also a good place to see deer, fox, and coyote.

Enter the woods again on the left and pass through an area of new growth where pine needles blanket the trail. Pines and cedars are among the first trees to regenerate cleared land. Almost all of the state's old-growth pines have long since been harvested. During colonial times pines were an extremely valuable tree, and those with a diameter greater than twenty-four inches and located within three miles of water were known as the King's Pines and reserved for use in the Royal Navy

From the fields at Tower Hill you can see Mount Wachusett, which Thoreau called the "blue wall."

The trail turns in a southerly direction passing in and out of the open field. It soon brings you to an area of bird feeders and three seats made of rough tree limbs where you can watch titmice, juncos, bluejays, nuthatches, and chickadees feed—all birds that stay with us through the winter. This area is known as the wildlife garden. Along with bird feeders are bat houses and a vernal pool—an active place in the spring when amphibians such as wood frogs and spring peepers return to these hatching spots to breed. Because vernal pools are low areas that usually hold water only during the spring months, there are no fish in them to eat the frog eggs and young.

Stay on the wide trail that heads farther into the forest dominated by large white pines. One winter's day I came upon three workers removing stumps from the trail here. One of them turned out to be the executive director of the Worcester County Horticultural Society, John Trexler. He told me that he had seen evidence of a bobcat here. In all my many hundreds of miles tramping through the woods I have yet to see one of these mysterious and elusive creatures. Perhaps my lucky sighting will come in February, which is breeding season, when the cats scream and yowl.

The trail emerges from the woods at the southern end of the property. Here you walk through the apple orchard on your way to the lawn garden, where hundreds of plants are labeled along a beautiful winding brick path. The parking lot is adjacent to this garden.

Total walking time for this outing is only about 50 minutes, but it takes me double that due to the frequent stops to admire the trees, shrubs, and flowers. (In April, May, and early June over 40,000 flower bulbs bloom here.)

Expect plenty of company if you come on a weekend between May and October. If you prefer solitude on the trails plan your trip during the week. From November to March the property is closed during the weekends and on holidays. The year-round hours are between 10:00 AM and 5:00 PM. Picnicking is permitted, but leave the pets at home. For more information on programs, garden tours, and special events call 508-869-6111. There is an admission charge for nonmembers of the Worcester County Horticultural Society.

Getting There

From Route 495 take Exit 25 for Route 290 west. Follow Route 290 for 5 miles to Exit 24, Church Street—Boylston/Northborough. Turn right at the end of the exit ramp and go toward Boylston. Go 3 miles (Church Street eventually turns into French Drive) and look for the Tower Hill Botanic Garden sign and entrance on the right, just before Route 70. (The entrance road is called Fuller Drive.)

From Boylston Center, go north on Route 70 for about a quarter of a mile, and turn right on French Drive. Entrance will be on the left a few feet up French Drive.

Gates Pond
Berlin
300 acres

Recommended walk: 2 $1/2$ miles, 1 hour

Finding a lake left in its natural state is rare indeed here in eastern Massachusetts. Here's a pond that doesn't have a single cottage on its shoreline, and the trail that circles it is open for all to enjoy. Gates Pond is a reservoir, managed by the Hudson Department of Public Works, and the only activities allowed are hiking and cross-country skiing. (Hudson and Berlin residents may apply for special fishing permits.)

Located just off Route 495 in Berlin, Gates Pond is easily accessible yet remains something of a secret. I've often hiked around the pond in the evening on my way home from business meetings in New Hampshire. The walk around the pond takes about forty-five minutes to an hour—just enough time to help you unwind after a busy day.

The path that leaves the parking area to the pond passes through a stately grove of red pines, white pines, and spruce. When you reach the pond you might be struck by its similarity to Walden Pond. They are roughly the same size and surrounded by woods, but at Gates Pond you won't have to contend with the hordes of visitors. In fact, I usually only see one or two other people there, at most.

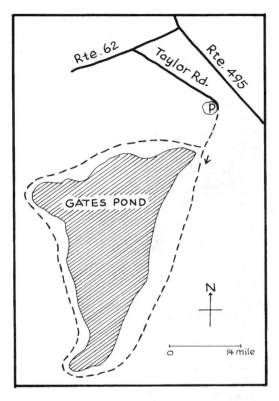

The path that circles the pond affords many areas
for viewing the water and its waterfowl; I once
watched a large cormorant dive for fish here. The
cormorant uses its webbed feet to propel itself underwater and, like the loon, it can stay beneath the
water's surface long enough to chase down most fish.
Its bill is quite powerful, and it has a small hook on

the end. Cormorants are frequently seen on lakes and rivers here in New England, but they are most common near the ocean.

A friend of mine once saw a bobcat prowling the shoreline of Gates Pond. This sighting is quite unusual because of the shy and elusive nature of these

A two-and-a-half mile trail circles the undeveloped shoreline of Gates Pond, where waterfowl and migratory birds can be seen.

strong fighters. They can hunt from trees or wait along a trail in ambush, and a large bobcat can even bring down a deer. Other prey include rabbits, mice, birds and their eggs, porcupines, squirrels, and other small animals. Bobcats are rare in heavily developed eastern Massachusetts and are more apt to be found in western Massachusetts and northern New England. It will be interesting to see how they fare now that they are competing with coyotes, a relative newcomer to the region.

On one walk around the pond I saw two white-tailed deer at the water's edge—perhaps they were taking a drink after raiding the nearby apple orchards of Berlin. Chipmunks are also quite common along the old stone walls and in the hemlock and cedar trees found along the water's edge.

Gates Pond is an excellent place to bring young children. It's impossible to get lost, the trail is fairly level, and for most folks living in the western suburbs it's an easy drive to get there.

Getting There

From Route 495 take Exit 26 to Route 62 west and head toward Berlin. After a short drive of a couple hundred feet look for Taylor Road on the left, just before a gas station. Drive all the way to the end of Taylor Road (0.7 mile) and park on the side of the road by the stone wall. Be sure not to block the entrance gate.

West of Boston

Charles River Peninsula
Needham
29 acres

Recommended walk: 1 mile, 30 minutes

The Charles River is known as the people's river or a "city river," but when hiking at the Charles River Peninsula it is easy to feel like this portion of the Charles lies a hundred miles from civilization. The reservation has rolling hills that slope gently down to the river, creating a pastoral scene that seems to come right off some impressionistic painter's easel. The fields are dotted with patches of bushes and trees where a variety of birds and animals make their home. Because of the abundance of small game, one or two red-tailed hawks always seem to be in the area.

There are no formal trails at Charles River Peninsula, but a walk around the perimeter of the field is recommended. (In summer the grass field is often overgrown.) The reservation is owned by The Trustees of Reservations, and at this time official access is by canoe only.

This area of the Charles is one of the best there is for wildlife along the entire river; only the Medfield-Natick area offers as much undeveloped land. The Charles River Peninsula was once a dairy farm and the

The lush meadow at the Charles River Peninsula is a good place to see small mammals. A variety of hawks also visit this open land along the Charles.

hay grown here today is still mowed. The section of the river immediately below the reservation is known as Red Wing Bay. This bay is just one of the many coves found between the South Natick Dam (located a few miles upriver) and the Cochrane Dam (just below Red Wing Bay). Waterfowl, such as the elusive wood duck, find the coves and setbacks much to their liking. Muskrat are sometimes observed prowling the river- bank or swimming in the coves. This is a great place to canoe, and the Metropolitan District Commission has recently built a canoe and cartop-boat launch off Fisher Street. Bring your fishing rod; the pickerel and largemouth-bass fishing is excellent.

When hiking the peninsula it's a good idea to bring binoculars and stop and scan the edges of the field every so often. That's how I once spotted an opossum shuffling along the ground. The opossum is the only marsupial native to North America and is actually related to the kangaroo. They are ordinarily

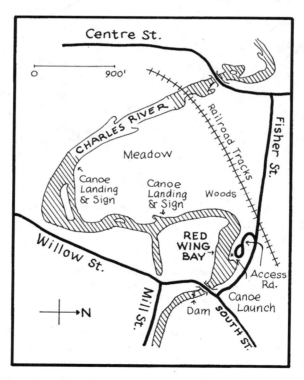

Made from mud, aquatic vegetation, and small branches, the muskrat lodge can be identified by its dome-shaped roof rising above the water's surface.

nocturnal animals; I have no idea why the one I saw was out in daylight.

Groundhogs (or woodchucks) are much easier to see; they come out to feed at various times during the day during the warm-weather months. (Watch out for the many woodchuck holes in the field when you walk.) They will eat just about any young plant that grows, and heaven help you if one finds your garden. Over the years I've had several tunnel right into my garden, eating dozens of different plant varieties— only the tomato plants escaped their voracious appetite. The tremendous amount of food groundhogs eat nourishes them during their winter hibernation. Their burrows usually have two entrances, several compartments, and can extend for several feet. A close inspection of a groundhog reveals that it looks very much like another rodent, the beaver, without a flat tail.

Besides the wood duck and red-tailed hawks I've seen a variety of birds here including turkey vultures, American kestrels, great blue herons, and I even once saw a passing osprey. But perhaps my favorite bird seen here is the little bluebird. Bluebirds favor open fields like the ones found at the Charles River Peninsula, and it is easy to attract these colorful songbirds by erecting a bluebird house. These must be built to exact specifications to attract bluebirds while thwarting more aggressive, larger birds. The entrance hole must be exactly 1.5 inches in diameter and there should not be a perch. The home should be placed on a pole about five feet up and the box should be left unpainted. Springtime is a great season to hike the peninsula because you not only get to see the bluebirds, but during April and May the flowering trees along the edge of the fields are in full bloom.

When visiting the area be sure to check out the rapids below the Cochrane Dam, found where South

Street intersects with Mill Street. If the water is high enough you might be able to watch the kayakers practice their maneuvers through the gates that are suspended just above the quick water. The power and grace that these kayakers display is worth the visit.

At this time the Charles River Peninsula can be reached by canoe only. It has two canoe landings along its wooded shoreline. There are a couple of ledge outcrops and one can view the river from a forested knoll.

Getting There

From Exit 17 off Route 128 go west on Route 135 (Dedham Avenue) about 0.8 mile (you will cross the Charles). Turn left onto South Street and drive 2.6 miles. Then turn right on Fisher Street just before the Cochrane Dam. Go 0.2 mile down Fisher Street and you will see the entrance to a canoe launching site on the left.

Elm Bank Reservation

Wellesley/Dover
182 acres

Recommended walk: 2 miles, 45 minutes
to an hour

Don't let the soccer fields fool you; this reservation
has miles of hiking trails through a forest that borders
the Charles River. The fact that up until recently these
wild acres could have been lost to development only
makes the property that much more special. Elm
Bank passed from various private owners until the
1970s when the state took over. The property still was
not safe from bulldozers and concrete until ownership was passed to the Metropolitan District Commission in 1991. The MDC will continue to manage Elm
Bank as a park, open to all. Activities found here
include soccer in the ball fields, canoeing in the river,
picnicking, cross-country skiing, and of course hiking.

Elm Bank includes 182 acres, best described as a
mitten-shaped peninsula, surrounded by the Charles
River on three sides. Excellent wildlife-watching possibilities exist here with animals such as deer, raccoon, mink, and fox inhabiting the quiet woodlands.
Park Supervisor Rob McArthur has seen a good variety of bird life here including eastern screech owls,
northern saw-whet owls, and great horned owls. Rob
has also seen the uncommon pileated woodpecker,

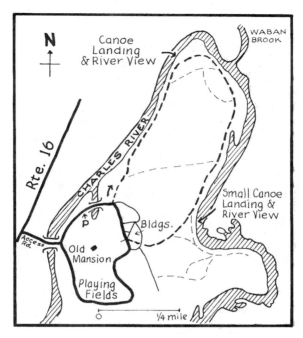

which has a brilliant red crest. There is good bird viewing along the Charles, where it's possible to see a number of wading birds such as great blue herons, black-crowned night herons, and green herons.

The reservation got its name back in the 1700s when elms were planted along the side of the river. The elms are gone, but the riverside trail is shaded by towering pines, hemlocks, maples, and oak trees. Some are quite old and massive, such as the hemlocks and spruce that line the main road.

When you enter the reservation you will cross a narrow scenic bridge over the Charles. The road then makes a rough circle around acres of open space that include the ball fields, hills, and some of the older buildings that were once part of this former estate. It is worth walking through the open center of the property to view the large old trees, including beech, sugar maple, and crimson maple. The small grassy hilltop is an excellent place to picnic.

Near this hilltop, at the center of the road that circles the property, is a boarded-up mansion. Although the once-lavish gardens are now crowded with weeds, some of the ornamental trees can be seen near a fallen marble fountain. With a little imagination it is easy to recognize the opulence and beauty that once surrounded this property. In fact, there is much beauty still to be seen even as the landscape returns to its wild state.

The best hiking trail is the one that follows the river. To reach the beginning of the trail, drive almost completely around the perimeter road (it is a one-way road) until you see the river and a sign for the cartop-boat launch. Park here and then walk back up the road in the direction you just came from until you see an iron gate leading to a dirt road that follows the river—a large map and sign were recently placed here. (In the winter the canoe-launch parking is not always plowed. Additional parking can be found behind the administration buildings. Large signs point the way.) This marks the beginning of the river trail, which I think offers one of the finest river walks in the state. The path is wide and quite flat, making it an excellent place to take children for a walk, and in the winter the cross-country skiing is superb.

On the left side of the path are some enormous old white pines. Owls nest and roost in these trees during the day and then come out in the evening to start their night of hunting rabbits, mice, and other small animals. Look closely at the trail for deer tracks; deer use the banks along the Charles as their travel corridor and can be seen near the river from its source all the way to Dedham. It's hard to see deer unless you are out at daybreak or dusk, when they are active. However, chipmunks and red squirrels are active all day long, as are many of the woodland birds that call Elm Bank home.

The trail follows a small ridge along the edge of the river, offering glimpses of the water below through the foliage and needles of pines, hemlocks, maples, and oaks. There is also a scattering of dogwood, beech, rhododendron, white birch, and sassafras with their two- or three-pronged mitten-shaped leaves. Notice that beneath the hemlocks almost nothing can grow, partly because of their shade and also because of the acidity of the hemlocks' fallen needles.

About ten or fifteen minutes down the trail you will reach a sunny opening next to the river where there are good views both upstream and down. All is quiet except for crickets and the occasional canoeist paddling by. This section of the river is one of the best places for canoeing because of the extensive stretch of undeveloped shoreline. About a mile downstream from this area the river emerges from the woodlands and broadens into a number of coves surrounded by

Elm Bank has one of the finest riverside trails in the area, where you might see pileated woodpeckers, owls, otter, muskrat, raccoon, and various wading birds such as the green heron.

marshlands. The fishing is excellent for warm-water species, and a hiker could combine a ramble with some fishing by carrying his or her fishing rod to this opening on the trail. (I've found the best way to catch Charles River largemouth bass and pickerel is to use a rubber worm inched along the bottom or a diving-minnow-type plug such as a Rapala.)

Birdwatchers should take a few moments to sit by the river and scan its shoreline for the wading birds, such as the great blue heron, that stalk the shallows. On one of my visits I saw an American bittern here. These rather large birds (twenty-three inches in length) are said to be common, but few people see them as they tend to stay close to water. They are elusive birds, most active at dusk, that sometimes hide themselves by freezing with their heads pointed straight up. Spotting them is extremely difficult once they freeze as their coloring is mostly mottled brown with some white and blends in quite well with the trees and vegetation. Green herons are also seen along the river, and they are sometimes mistaken for bitterns.

The river views are usually full of color. In the spring the swamp maples have new growth and buds that are a deep reddish purple, while in the summer there are more flashes of purple from the purple loosestrife. This aquatic weed was brought over from Europe over a century ago, and while its colors are beautiful it is crowding out the native vegetation and altering the delicate balance of plant life along swamps and rivers throughout southern New England.

At the big bend in the river it is possible to see the mouth of Waban Brook. The brook descends from Lake Waban, which borders the beautiful campus of Wellesley College. Some hearty canoeists I know have traveled from the Charles up the brook all the way to the college. (If you do canoe this stretch of river, I recommend that you stay on the Charles, because the brook is narrow and choked with vegetation.)

It is possible to make a complete loop of the peninsula by continuing to walk the river trail as it follows the Charles downstream. (The trails you are on were old carriage roads, and because the trails are not well marked it is easy to get confused.) About thirty minutes into the hike you will reach a small canoe landing (or ten-foot opening in the trees along the river) that offers a river view. The landing is fifty yards past a large boulder on the left. The trail that loops back to the main access road forks off to the right just opposite the canoe landing and passes a steel gate five minutes into the walk. (You will know you went too far on the river trail when you see that it begins to narrow considerably.)

Total hiking time is about forty-five minutes to an hour. By exploring side trails you can extend your hike considerably. Be careful to avoid the poison ivy that grows in profusion in these woods. Elm Bank is closed to the public on Mondays and Tuesdays. Wednesday through Sunday it is open from 9:00 AM to dusk.

Getting There

From Route 128 take Exit 21 and follow Route 16 west 4.9 miles. The entrance to Elm Bank is in Wellesley and will be on your left, marked by a small blue sign (about 0.4 mile before South Natick Center).

Noanet Woodlands

591 acres

Dover

Recommended walk: about 3 1/2 miles,
1 3/4 hour

Diversity of terrain is what makes Noanet so special;
swamplands, brooks, millponds, a waterfall, upland
forests, and a 387-foot peak can all be found here.
These features provide excellent nature study as well
as hiking, jogging, and cross-country skiing on the
reservation's extensive network of trails. The variety
of terrain, coupled with the fact the property abuts
privately owned Hale Reservation (1,200 acres) and
Powisset Farm (105 acres), makes this an ideal
wildlife refuge.

Noanet Woodlands has so many trails, many
unnamed, that it is easy to get lost. The map shown
in this book does not show every trail in the reservation but instead focuses on the trails that lead from
the parking lot to Noanet Peak. The main trails have
color-coded discs fastened to trees, and our review
will mention the appropriate colors for the trails
described. (The walk to the ponds is relatively flat,
while our walk to the peak gets quite steep in spots.)

Our walk begins by following the Caryl Trail,
which is the main trail leaving the parking lot. Follow
the sign at the back end of the parking lot that points

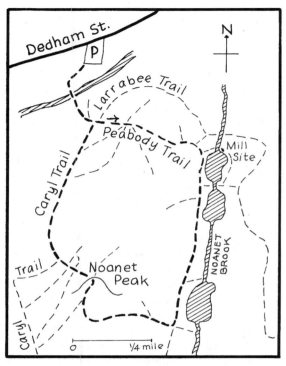

the way to Noanet Woodlands. The trail first goes through the playground of Caryl Park (owned by the town of Dover) and then enters the pine and oak forest. Caryl Trail is marked by yellow discs. It heads in a southerly direction, passing through a low-lying area where the trail sometimes gets muddy. After walking a little less than half a mile you will pass an unmarked trail on the left, and then three or four minutes later you will come to a split in the trail where a contributions box has been placed on a post. Go left here. About twenty feet farther the trail splits again. To the left is the Larrabee Trail and to the right is the Peabody Trail. Take the Peabody Trail, marked by blue discs. About five minutes down the Peabody Trail you will come to an open area with a trail coming in on the right. Stay straight on the Peabody Trail. A few feet after that the trail forks, and you should continue on the Peabody Trail by bearing left. The trail now hugs the edge of a ridge.

After about a quarter mile you will see a sparkling waterfall cascading from the old millpond on the left side of the trail. This was once the site of the Dover Union Iron Company, which operated from 1815 into the 1830s. The Trustees of Reservations, which owns Noanet, says that "Noanet Brook was too small a stream to support the ironworks and the company went out of business." The original dam was destroyed by flooding in 1876 but was reconstructed by Amelia Peabody in 1954, who later bequeathed the land to the Trustees.

The holding ponds above the dam are a perfect place to sit and have lunch to the sound of falling water and singing birds. Painted turtles, frogs, and bluegills inhabit the various ponds and wetlands. The setting is made complete by the large pines, oaks, maples, and beech that surround the ponds.

After exploring the mill site continue on the Peabody Trail (blue discs) as it passes between Noanet Brook far on the left and forested slopes to the right. The trail leads in a southerly direction and you should follow it for about $3/8$ of a mile. Just

Noanet Brook spills from the sluice opening of the dam below the millponds. This was once the site of the Dover Union Iron Company, but now is home to a wide assortment of wild creatures.

beyond the third pond you will come to a four-way trail intersection. To reach Noanet Peak take the unnamed trail on the right, which climbs the hill. After about 50 yards the trail bears to the left (the path straight ahead peters out at an area of exposed rock on the hillside). By bearing left you are now circling the peak, rather than making a frontal climb. Yet still this trail is quite steep in spots. Follow this trail for about 10 minutes and by bearing to the right at the next intersection you will reach the summit in only a couple more minutes of walking. At the top of the peak is an excellent view of the Boston skyline and hills to the east. Powissett Peak, part of the nearby Hale Reservation, can also be seen. In the fall, the hilltop is a good place to see migrating hawks wing their way south.

From Noanet Peak, retrace your steps for about fifty feet then bear right downhill on an unnamed trail that descends the hill to the west. Stay straight on this trail until it meets with the Caryl Trail, marked by the yellow discs (about a five-minute walk from the summit). Bear right on the Caryl Trail. After ten minutes you pass homes on the left side of the trail, and then it's another fifteen minutes on the Caryl Trail to the parking area.

More ambitious hikers may wish to hike through the southern end of the property. Although I have not hiked beyond Noanet Peak, the reservation's trail guide shows that you could take a long walk along the perimeter of the property, by first following the Caryl Trail to the south. The Caryl Trail then hooks up with the Larrabee Trail, which follows a northerly course back toward the parking area where it reconnects with the Caryl Trail. This is quite a long hike; I'd guess it's at least six miles, so bring water if you go. (The reservation is so large that even when the these less-popular trails.) There is another new entrance trail on the east side of the parking lot which also leads to the mill site.

On weekends and holidays a ranger is on duty. (You should ask the ranger about trail conditions and any recent changes made.) There is no entrance fee. An excellent map can be purchased from the ranger, who can give you some great hiking tips. Fishing is allowed in Noanet Brook and the cross-country skiing is excellent when there's snow. The reservation is well suited for older children—they will love the waterfall and the view from Noanet Peak, and there are plenty of intriguing rock formations for a child and parent to explore.

Getting There

From Route 128, take Exit 17, Route 135 west. Drive 0.7 mile. Turn left on South Street just after crossing the Charles River. Go 1.1 miles on South Street and turn left on Chestnut Street. Follow Chestnut Street 0.4 mile to its end, and turn right on Dedham Street immediately after crossing the Charles River. Continue 2 miles to the entrance and parking lots on left at Caryl Park.

From Dover Center, take Dedham Street eastward for 0.6 mile to park entrance on the right.

Peters Reservation
Dover
91 acres

Recommended walk: 2 miles, 1 hour

With 2,047 feet of frontage on the Charles you would expect the Peters Reservation to have superior wildlife and birdwatching, and you won't be disappointed. Muskrat, otter, raccoon, weasel, deer, kingfishers, hawks, great blue herons, ruffed grouse, and a wide assortment of waterfowl can be seen. Because so few people come here, the chances of spotting wildlife are good.

Peters Reservation is accessible only by canoe. The reservation is located on the Dover side of the Charles River near the Bridge Street bridge. A small parking area serves as an excellent canoe launch. It is only a short (1/8-mile) paddle downstream to reach the landing, which is marked by a sign on the right-hand side of the river.

The canoe landing is a good spot for bass fishing or just plain relaxing. It is adjacent to a dark forest of red pines. In the summer, a lush undergrowth of ferns give the woods a tropical look. When I visited here in late March I enjoyed the combination of colors displayed along the river. The sun was low in the sky and highlighted the golds and browns of the marsh grass, and the swamp maples had a touch of

The Peters Reservation protects over 2,000 feet of frontage along the tranquil Charles River. Heron, duck, raptor, deer, raccoon, weasel, and other wildlife can be seen here.

red at the end of each twig where new growth had begun.

A creature that often dwells near the water's edge is the weasel, both ermines and the larger long-tailed weasels. They hunt for frogs, snakes, and bird nests; I once heard a bird screaming here and looked up to see a weasel running away from the nest, which was located in the brush along the riverbank. Another animal seen along the Charles is the white-tailed deer. In fact, their population may be at an all-time high, and it is not uncommon to see deer browsing in the roadside fields in Dover and Sher-

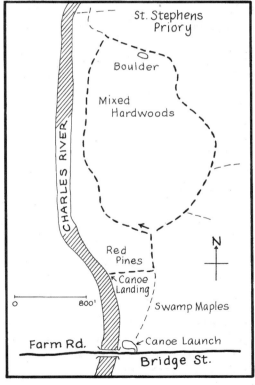

born. Deer will feed on a wide variety of plants, usually the tips of buds and shrubs.

From the canoe landing, follow the trail away from the banks of the Charles and then turn left where it intersects with the main trail. You can make a loop of the property by turning left at the next intersection. This narrow path runs parallel to the Charles and leads you out of the red pines and into a mixed hardwood forest. Oak, hickory, and Dexter rhododendron begin to appear. After about twenty to twenty-five minutes the narrow trail you are on intersects with the main trail, and by turning right and bearing right past two more side trails you will eventually reach the spot where the narrow trail first left the main trail, back near the red pines and the landing. Along the way you will pass a large boulder on the right that has a smaller boulder resting on top of it, making a most unusual sight.

The white pines, red pines, and hemlocks of Peters Reservation are habitat features preferred by the red squirrel. They not only make their nests at the top of these trees but they eat their seeds as well. Winter food caches of seeds are buried in the ground and can contain over a bushel of food. Suprisingly, they also eat insects, birds, and their eggs, and have even been known to kill a young rabbit or gray squirrel.

The red squirrel is quite swift, running from limb to limb and jumping from tree to tree. And it's a good thing—they are hunted by owls, hawks, fishers, minks, and bobcats. On the ground they face the threat of red foxes, gray foxes (which can also climb trees), and coyotes. Even in the water the squirrel is vulnerable if it happens to have the misfortune of swimming in the wrong place; snapping turtles will snatch them, as will large fish such as pike.

This is one of the prime areas on the Charles for seeing great blue herons. Be sure not to disturb the birds as they feed along the banks—if you canoe straight down the river and don't veer off toward the birds, chances are they will freeze and then resume hunting once you have passed.

Perhaps because the reservation is only a few years old it receives few visitors; I've rarely seen another person hiking there. While you are in the area, be sure to drive up Farm Road into Sherborn to see the beautiful country scenes of stone walls, farms, and a historic graveyard found just above the Charles. It's a perfect road for biking, and the Charles River, both upstream and down, provides excellent canoeing here. Leave one car near the South Natick dam, and then drive back to Bridge Street to launch. Your float downstream will take you past Peters Reservation and Broadmoor Wildlife Sanctuary. You will also pass by a praying woman statue and beneath a lovely footbridge that spans the river.

Getting There

From Route 128, take Exit 21 to Route 16 west. Travel 6.3 miles into South Natick. Turn left on South Street and go to its end (1.8 miles). Turn left on Farm Road and go 1.2 miles. When you cross the Charles, the canoe launch area will be on your left. (Paddle downstream ⅛ mile and the landing will be on your right.)

Broadmoor Wildlife Sanctuary

Natick
608 acres (770 acres including
conservation restrictions)

Recommended walk: 3 miles, $1^1/_2$–2 hours

Broadmoor is a sanctuary rich in both wildlife and history. In 1651, the entire South Natick area was the scene of an experimental arrangement between Native Americans and the early settlers. The Reverend John Eliot and a group of "praying Indians" (Christian converts) established a community here that was to be very similar to the white man's style of living. The community was only a partial success, with problems ranging from the imprisonment of the Native Americans during King Philip's War to the cultural difficulties that might be expected.

While Broadmoor has no visible signs of this community, there are the fascinating remains of a gristmill that the Native Americans allowed to be operated and owned here. Thomas Swaain's mill was built in the 1690s and was powered by the waters of Indian Brook and the holding pond or millpond. Today you can see not only the pond, but also two of the enormous millstones as well.

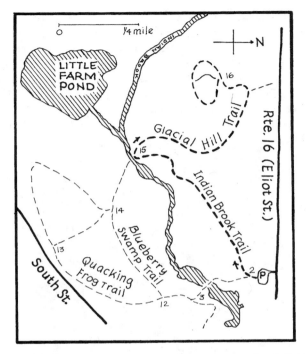

Broadmoor has become a very popular hiking spot because of its diversity of terrain and wildlife. At the nature center building you can pick up a copy of an excellent sanctuary map that details its nine miles of trails. The trails have color-coded markers, with blue taking you away from the parking lot and yellow leading you back.

The most scenic area is at the eastern end of the property, where the Mill Pond–Marsh Trail takes you by the wildlife pond and the mill sites and the Charles River Trail leads down along the river. Wildlife is abundant here, with fairly regular sightings of wood ducks, painted turtles, kingfishers, great blue herons, and hawks. Usually unseen, but also inhabiting these woods, are great horned owls, raccoons, fox, deer, and even river otter. In addition to Indian Brook you can see the small waterfalls,

River otter, mink, and muskrat live in the Broadmoor wetlands. (Paul Rezendes photo)

stone foundations of an old sawmill, and the mill-stones. The hemlock trees not only shade this area, but they give the stream an enchanting and mysterious look, even on a sunny day. Across South Street, the Charles River Trail follows the river for a half-mile and tupelo trees line the riverbank, with the more common pines and oaks.

I find some of the less-frequented trails equally interesting if not quite as scenic. And even when the parking area is full, the trails leading to the western end of the property rarely receive more than a few hikers. One such trail is the Indian Brook Trail, which leads to the even more secluded Glacial Hill Trail. Begin your walk by registering at the visitor's center and then turning right a few feet down the main trail onto Indian Brook Trail. The beginning of Indian Brook Trail passes through a beautiful open field where kestrels, kingbirds, mockingbirds, cedar waxwings, and indigo buntings can be seen in addition to a couple of resident groundhogs. Soon the trail leads into a wooded area of oaks on the right and Indian Brook Swamp on the left.

The wetlands here are the scene of an exciting new wildlife development—beavers. Elissa Landre, director of Broadmoor, told me that beavers moved into the Indian Brook Swamp in 1989. For lovers of the Charles River watershed, this is big news indeed, as these are apparently the first beavers to inhabit the area in many years. Landre says that the beaver are "shy and difficult to see; I've only seen them once, and that was at dusk when one of them slapped its tail on the water." She says these beavers have built their homes by burrowing into the bank rather than building a lodge. They have constructed a small dam, however, which can be seen at the junction of Indian Brook Trail and Glacial Hill Trail near signpost 15.

Beavers were extirpated from the entire state around 1860. Their valuable pelts made them the focus of heavy trapping. It wasn't until recently that the beaver has regained a foothold in the state, primarily through the reintroduction efforts of the Massachusetts Division of Fisheries and Wildlife. A biologist with that agency, Tom Decker, told me that beavers are expanding all over the state now, even to the point of being a nuisance in some areas. But that's a small price to pay to have these fascinating creatures back, building their ponds and creating new wetlands. In fact, Elissa Landre is hoping the dying trees in the newly flooded beaver pond at Broadmoor will attract nesting great blue herons, which prefer to make their nests at these impoundments.

Continue your walk by turning right at signpost 15, which will put you on the Glacial Hill Trail, heading northwest. Glacial Hill Trail winds its way through the oaks for about a mile before reaching the little hill or drumlin formed by glaciers. The hill is a doughnut-shaped glacial deposit rising up from the swampy forest below. The trail runs along the top of the hill, forming a small loop before bringing you back to the main path.

From here you can retrace your steps back to the parking lot, or try crossing Indian Brook where Glacial Hill Trail meets Indian Brook Trail. You can then take Blueberry Swamp Trail toward the east. Stay on the

Blueberry Swamp Trail by bearing left at signpost 14, which will lead you to the Mill Pond–March Trail. Bear left at 12 and 3 and you will be back at the parking lot. I often see ruffed grouse near the Blueberry Swamp Trail, and one time I saw a red fox.

The walk to the glacial hill and back is about three miles, so plan on spending two or three hours walking and exploring one of the Massachusetts Audubon Society's best properties.

Another little-known section of the sanctuary is Little Farm Pond, just over the Natick line in Sherborn. To reach this pond drive about a mile or two west on Route 16 from the main parking lot. Turn left onto Lake Street and go about a mile to Farm Road. Turn left onto Farm Road and look for a small parking area on the left side of the road (about a hundred yards from the intersection of Lake Street and Farm Road). From here you can hike down the dirt road to the pond and explore some unmarked trails along its west side. This is a special place, quiet and rich with wildlife and unusual plant life such as the carnivorous sundew and pitcher plant.

Getting There

From Route 128 take Exit 21 to Route 16 west. Travel 7 miles into South Natick. The parking lot and signs welcoming you to Broadmoor will be on your left.

The sanctuary is located on Route 16 (280 Eliot Street), 1.8 miles west of South Natick Center. The sanctuary is open every day except Monday, and there is a modest admission fee for nonmembers.

Rocky Narrows
Sherborn
150 acres

Recommended walk: 1 miles, 35 minutes
(accessible by canoe)

The towering hemlocks and pines anchored on the steep hillside slopes of Rocky Narrows are more reminiscent of northern New England than eastern Massachusetts. This rugged terrain, coupled with the fact that the reservation can only be reached by canoe, gives the hiker the feeling he or she is in a region much more remote than Sherborn, just a half-hour drive from downtown Boston.

Rocky Narrows lies on the west bank of the Charles River and can be reached by canoe launching at the Bridge Street bridge on the Dover-Sherborn line. (It is anticipated that there will soon be foot access to Rocky Narrows from a small parking lot to be built near the intersection of Lake Street and Forest Street in Sherborn.) Paddle upstream about three-quarters of a mile and look for a large welcoming sign on the right-hand side of the river. There is a nice grassy landing here. If you plan on going for a long hike, bring a lock and chain to secure your canoe to a tree. Always bring bug spray and a jug of water.

I have brought my two young children with me on many of my hikes, but this is not one of them. The

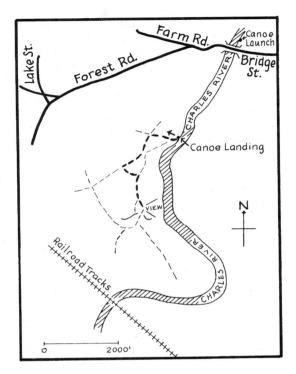

reservation is quite hilly and since the car is parked far downstream, I think it's too remote for children, especially if you happen to get caught in a thunderstorm. It is also easy to get lost here as the trails are not well marked.

Rocky Narrows is one of the few places on the Charles where steep granite ledges come down to the water's edge. The area has been known historically as the Gates of the Charles, and I've also seen it referred to as Dingle Hole Narrows and simply the Narrows. The narrowest portion of the river actually lies a short way upstream from the reservation's landing, but at no place are there any churning rapids as the name might suggest.

At one time a fort stood on a promontory near here, high above the river, as a settler's defensive refuge against the Native Americans. Unfortunately, it was the natives who needed to defend themselves against the encroachment of white settlers. Two battles were fought just a few miles upstream in 1676, one at South End Pond in Millis and another at the town of Medfield. Those battles, fought during King Philip's War, marked the beginning of the end for the Indians and allowed the settlers to take more land. Today, Rocky Narrows is owned by The Trustees of Reservations and is open for all to enjoy.

The most interesting feature at the reservation is a cliff overlook that offers a hawk's-eye view of the river and marshes below. To reach the cliff, take the main trail that leads directly away from the Charles. Walk about 300 feet to the first four-way intersection of trails and go left. This trail passes through a low-lying area and then by a stone wall on the left. (The trail briefly passes from The Trustees of Reservations property into the Sherborn Town Forest.) About 100 feet after the stone wall you will see a trail leading uphill on your left—look for a yellow-painted marker on a tree next to the trail. Turn left onto this trail and follow it as it climbs a hill. You will walk in almost total shade beneath oaks, pines, and hemlocks. Chatty red squirrels can be heard amid the dense branches of the hemlocks.

On a June visit here, I surprised a ruffed grouse and her chicks. Over the years, I've seen a number of mother grouses do strange things to distract attention away from their chicks. Sometimes they creep around feigning injury, while other times they make a hissing noise. But this grouse made a series of squawks and shrieks so unearthly they made the hair on my neck stand straight up. It was a good ruse. I forgot all about the chicks for a moment, and that's all it takes for them to camouflage themselves against the brown forest floor.

When you climb this trail as it hugs a ridge high above the river valley, you can't help but be impressed by the beauty of the grand old hemlock trees. Beneath their sweeping branches is a dark forest almost void of undergrowth due to the lack of sun. Where the sun does filter through, you may notice bees hovering in its warmth. Occasionally you can get a glimpse of the Charles River far below.

After about a ten-minute walk, mostly uphill, you will reach the cliff with the great view. This is a fine place to sit and rest or have lunch. There is a healthy population of white-tailed deer that roam along the river corridor; you might just see one as you scan the meadows below. You have an even better chance of spotting red-tailed hawks and great blue herons—they use the river as their flight path. I was once sitting on this ledge when I saw a red-tailed hawk fly by with a chipmunk in its talons. Another hawk trailed behind screeching. Was the second

From the overlook at Rocky Narrows one looks down upon a secluded meadow and the Charles River beyond.

hawk going to be allowed to share in the meal or was he screeching from jealousy?

Because there are so many confusing trails, I advise visitors to return to their canoe by retracing their steps. You might want to purchase a topographical map of the area to give you a better look at the

Charles, the reservation, and the many scenic back roads that lead through Dover and Sherborn.

I suggest you try your hand at the bass fishing in the Charles. Fish the shady banks using a Rapala Minnow or white spinnerbait. There are some nice-sized bass here, as well as pickerel; please release your catch to keep the fishing good for the next generation.

Getting There

As funds become available, The Trustees of Reservations plan to build an entrance to Rocky Narrows on Forest Road. For updated information, call the Trustees at 617-821-7977.

By Canoe

From Route 128 take Exit 21 to Route 16 west. Travel 6.3 miles into South Natick and turn left on South Street. Go to the end of South Street (1.8 miles) and turn left on Farm Road. Go 1.2 miles on Farm Road, and when you cross the Charles a canoe launch will be immediately on your left. Paddle upstream about a mile.

From Route 27 in Sherborn (near the Medfield line) you can reach the canoe launch by taking Forest Road eastward to a right on Farm Road. As Farm Road crosses the Charles the canoe launch is immediately on the left.

Rocky Woods Reservation
Medfield
490 acres

Recommended walks: Southern Section
3 $^1/_2$ miles, 1 $^1/_2$ hours; Cedar Hill: 1 mile,
30 minutes; Hemlock Knoll Nature Trail:
1 mile, 30–40 minutes

Rocky Woods is one of the larger properties owned by The Trustees of Reservations, and it offers a wide choice of year-round recreational activities. (Because it is so large, three walks are described here.) The focal point of the reservation is five-acre Chickering Lake, where there is catch-and-release fishing during the warmer months. Picnic tables and grills are scattered about the shoreline.

Of all the activities my favorite is still the hiking—or cross-country skiing in winter—on the miles of trails that pass by secluded swamps, through dense forests, and over scenic hilltops. The name Rocky Woods is appropriate; the land is a series of uneven ridges with many rocky outcrops including Whale Rock, which looks like the back of a whale rising from the forest floor. The reservation is rich in wildlife, and early morning hikers are often treated to a sighting of a fox, partridge, or a great blue heron wading in one of the ponds.

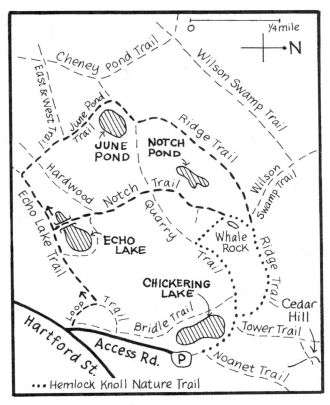

Because Rocky Woods is a large property with various trail-access points from the entrance road, I've split my hikes between the southern section and the northern section. The northern section includes Cedar Hill and the Hemlock Knoll self-guided nature trail, the better trail for children.

Southern Section

This hike, through the property's southern area, takes about an hour and a half. Just after you turn off Hartford Street onto the Access Road is a small parking area on the left where you will find Loop Trail. Take this wide, well-maintained path of crushed stone for a short distance until its junction with Echo Lake Trail. Tall oaks provide plenty of shade on a hot summer's day, and mountain laurel and rhododendron can be seen scattered in the forest understory. Maple, dogwood, white pine, hemlock, and sassafras can also be seen along the path. During August, the scent of the fragrant flowering sweet pepperbush spices the air. The pepperbush's white flowers add a nice visual contrast to the wall of green foliage bordering the trail. When you reach Echo Lake continue straight on the main path, which skirts the shallow waters of this small pond. Stop for a moment on the wooden footbridge to look for frogs, turtles, and waterfowl. Then continue back on the main trail, which heads in a southwesterly direction. This trail is excellent for cross-country skiing—there are just enough slopes for excitement and the trail is wide.

At the next intersection turn right. This path soon passes by an even smaller pond called June Pond, which is all but dry in midsummer. Just after you spot June Pond take a right at the next intersection. This is the 0.7-mile Ridge Trail. You will notice that both the trees and the terrain begin to change here. Beech trees and birch trees begin to appear and granite boulders, dropped during the retreat of the glaciers, fill the woods. Now you know the origin of the name Rocky Woods.

Walk along Ridge Trail until you come to Hardwood Notch Trail on the right (a sign will say intersection 5). Take this right. Soon you will see the giant Whale Rock stretching out like a beached whale along the trail on your left.

Continue down Hardwood Notch Trail, keeping watch for a trail that goes to the left beneath a sign on a tree that says "lookout point." (The lookout is a narrow view that can be reached after a four- or five-minute walk.) Continuing down Hardwood Notch Trail, you pass tiny Notch Pond on your right, then cross the intersection with Quarry Trail. About 400 feet after this intersection, look for a small path on the left that leads back to Echo Lake where you can cross the footbridge and turn left onto Echo Lake Trail to return to your car.

Northern Section

Cedar Hill Hike

Lying north of Chickering Lake, the exposed ridge line of Cedar Hill can be reached in a short, fifteen-minute hike. There are a number of different views to be seen, and there is nothing quite as peaceful as gazing out over the valleys and hills as cool breezes whisper through the cedars. While I was sitting there I couldn't help but think that this hilltop looked like rattlesnake country. There still a handful of rattlesnakes left in New England, but it would be a rare thing indeed for a hiker ever to see one.

Cedar Hill can be reached by taking the Chickering Pond Trail to the Tower Trail. As you walk up Tower Trail you will see numerous smaller paths leading up to the ridge on the right.

Hemlock Knoll Nature Trail

In addition to the southern hike, Rocky Woods includes the Hemlock Knoll Nature Trail. The Trustees of Reservations sell an excellent twenty-four-page guidebook for the Hemlock Knoll Nature Trail. The trail has eighteen numbered markers at various trees, plants, and rocks that correspond with the detail in the guidebook. It is an excellent way for both children and adults to learn about nature.

The trail begins at the north side of Chickering Lake and forms a loop in the woods of about one mile. Take a good look around the shoreline of the lake before you begin—many times I've seen a great blue heron hunting there. A few times I've even seen the giant bird perched in a pine tree above the water. Kingfishers can also be seen here, and it's thrilling to watch them dive from their perch and into the water to grab a small fish.

Chickering Lake is a very good spot to take the kids fishing. Sunfish are relatively easy to catch with worms or other bait. And one never knows when the largemouth bass might be hungry, so bring some lures (all fish must be released).

Hemlock Trail is well marked and well maintained, which makes it a great hike for youngsters. At the intersection of the Tower Trail and the Ridge Trail, follow the Ridge Trail to begin your walk. One

A young hiker tries the trail along Chickering Lake.

of the most interesting features is the "minicanyon" at marker 6. The passage was formed during the time of the glaciers when a stream passed through here.

After about a half-mile on the Ridge Trail turn left on Hardwood Notch Trail. It takes you to the massive Whale Rock where the kids will enjoy climbing. After Whale Rock, the trail begins its return back to Chickering Lake. Turn left at the first turn after Whale Rock, then about 400 feet farther turn left again onto Quarry Trail. On the way back you will pass the remains of a quarry where in the early 1900s blocks of stone were cut and hauled out by horses and oxen. Drill marks can still be seen in the rocks. From here it is a short walk back to the parking lot. Witch hazel, sassafras, shagbark hickory, and dogwood trees can all be seen in the last quarter-mile.

It is interesting to note that the ridge you have just been walking separates the Charles River watershed from the Neponset River watershed. Both of these rivers were used extensively by the Native Americans for travel, and artifacts have been found in numerous sites along their banks.

Getting There

From the intersection of Routes I-95/128 and 109 (Exit 16B on I-95), take Route 109 west 5.7 miles through Westwood to Hartford Street in Medfield. Take a right (hairpin turn) onto Hartford Street. Follow it 0.6 mile to the entrance and parking lot on the left.

From the intersection of Routes 27 and 109 in Medfield, take Route 109 east. Bear left on Hartford Street 0.6 mile to the entrance on the left.

There is an admission fee on weekends and holidays, with a ranger on duty at these times.

Fork Factory Brook Reservation
Medfield
135 acres

Recommended walk: 1 $1/2$ miles, 45 minutes

Fork Factory Brook Reservation (the name comes from a nearby old iron mill that made pitchforks) is situated across the street from Rocky Woods Reservation, and while Rocky Woods is fairly well known, only a handful of locals even know that Fork Factory exists. On a recent spring afternoon I peeked into the parking lot at Rocky Woods and saw too many cars for my liking so I simply hiked the trails of Fork Factory, where I didn't see another person. These trails are not quite as scenic as Rocky Woods, but they travel along a ridge above a secluded wooded swamp where the birds and animals see few hikers. (There is no formal trail system here as there is at Rocky Woods.)

The entrance to Fork Factory Brook Reservation is hidden at the far end of a field just a few feet to the south and across the entrance from the Rocky Woods parking area. Perhaps this hidden entrance is why few people even know that Fork Factory, owned by The Trustees of Reservations, is open to the public. (Plans are in the works to erect a sign marking the entrance.) The field along Hartford Street is an excel-

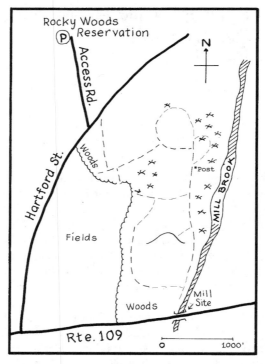

lent area for spotting wildlife such as harrier hawks, red-tailed hawks, and foxes that hunt for mice. Walk along the edge of the field (where pumpkins are grown) until you reach a wide path that cuts through a pine grove. Small black spruce trees, which are unusual for this area, can be seen on the side of the trail as nuthatches fly from tree to tree.

Heading straight into the woods and bearing left at the first intersection, the path skirts swampy areas

120   West of Boston

that are thick with low-lying trees and more unusual plants such as leatherleaf, pitcher plants, and wild cranberries. This woodland swamp abuts the large watershed of Mill Brook. White-tailed deer have made this impenetrable swamp their home, and because the trail sees so few visitors it's possible to spot a deer at dawn or dusk. At the eastern end of the trail you can go either right or left; to the right is a trail on a ridge line that eventually brings you to a rocky hill with a trail climbing the hill from the north side. The hill is small enough to climb with children, and for once there is no graffiti marking its exposed ledges, as there is on so many of the state's hilltops. I prefer to make this hike in the fall when the leaves are off the trees and you can see through the swamp better.

The north side of the reservation also features a trail hugging a ridge line where you can see the burrows of a number of animals such as fox, skunk, and woodchuck that like to dig into hillsides. You will also pass an old cellar hole and a granite post, a reminder of how this area was once cleared for farming.

An equally interesting place to poke around is the area off Route 109 where Mill Brook crosses the road. If you look closely you can see an old sluiceway where the water once raced out of the dammed millponds. For some unknown reason Mill Brook used to be called Tubwreck Brook; I can just picture a bathtub spinning out of control down the brook. The water that raced through the sluiceway is what powered the mills that were first used to grind corn or saw lumber. Later the mills were expanded into factories such as textile, iron (including those pitchforks), and paper.

A rocky promontory at Fork Factory Brook Reservation.

In a recent conversation I had with Tom Foster, the southeast regional supervisor for The Trustees of Reservations, we compared notes on the wildlife we'd seen here. Tom described how he once saw what he thinks was a coyote in the field chasing mice. The animal was too far away to make positive identification, but whether it was a coyote or fox, Tom said it was a sight to behold as the animal sprang up in the air to pounce on the fleeing mice. Chances are that it was a coyote, as these animals continue to expand their range, moving from Canada southward. Coyotes have even been sighted on Cape Cod. However, they do a good job of avoiding humans, preferring the cover of darkness for most of their activity.

When hunting, coyotes often do so in pairs or small groups, traveling in single file. Their main food source is deer carrion, but they prey on fawns, birds, mice, rabbits, frogs, snakes, turtles, fish, crayfish, berries, and fruits. They will slowly stalk a rabbit and then pounce on it, grabbing it by the throat. If a group of coyotes is chasing an animal they will do so in relays, much like a pack of wolves. The coyote is quite swift and can run in bursts up to forty-three miles an hour, although when hunting in packs and using the relay method they can simply wear their prey down through this relentless pursuit.

Coyotes are larger than foxes; large males can weigh up to fifty pounds (some wolf genes have been found in eastern coyotes). Their primary color is gray, with some brown around the muzzle. They are social animals and will howl for both pleasure and as a warning to other coyotes. When traveling in groups they will sometimes make irregular howls or a yipping sound.

Getting There

From Route 128, take Exit 16 onto Route 109 west. Drive 5.7 miles through Westwood to Hartford Street in Medfield. Take a right (hairpin turn) onto Hartford Street. Follow it 0.6 mile to the entrance of Rocky Woods. Park and walk back across Hartford Street and enter Fork Factory Brook Reservation through the field. (Use caution when crossing Hartford Street—the traffic is often heavy and fast.)

Henry L. Shattuck Reservation

Medfield
225 acres

Recommended walk: 1 3/4 miles, 45 minutes

Shattuck Reservation has all the ingredients to support a variety of wildlife: 1.25 miles of frontage along
the Charles River, broad wetlands, and upland
forests of white pine, oak, and red maples that lie
close to the water. Dogwoods and crab apple trees
have been planted to improve the habitat for wildlife.
Like the Noon Hill Reservation next door, Shattuck
Reservation receives few visitors, which allows for
better wildlife viewing along with peaceful hiking
and cross-country skiing.

The reservation lies between the Charles River to
the west and Causeway Street to the east. Causeway
Street is a seldom-used dirt road that runs along the
edge of the great Millis-Medfield Marsh. Be sure to
walk or drive northward up this narrow road to
view the confluence of the Stop River and the
Charles. A picturesque wooden bridge passes over
the Stop River offering views of the marshlands.

Access to Shattuck Reservation can be gained
through three different trails that run from Causeway
Street toward the river. The trail closest to the Stop

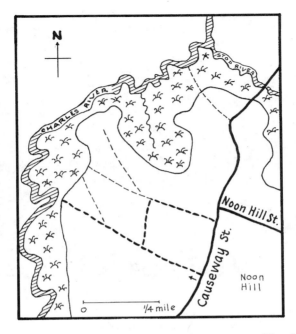

River (its entrance does not have a green gate like the other two entrances) goes directly to the Charles by passing through a short wooded area and then through the marsh. The trail ends at the water's edge where the remains of an old bridge can be seen. It's a quiet spot to sit and watch the slow, dark waters of the Charles go by.

The other two trails go through hilly wooded terrain where deer can occasionally be seen if you are lucky (and quiet). In the springtime pink lady's slippers and an assortment of other wildflowers grow

A peaceful winter scene by the marsh and river at the secluded Shattuck Reservation.

along the wooded paths. Red fox use the same trails we do for ease of traveling in search of small game. The river itself is home to muskrat, otter, and mink. Otter and mink are difficult to get a glimpse of, but the muskrat is rather common as it prowls the river's edge in search of aquatic plants to eat. The prolific muskrat is a food source for mink as well as owls and foxes. Great horned owls have been seen gliding through the reservation's tall white pines. Look for great blue herons with their enormous seven-foot wingspan using the Charles as their highway as they search for food or travel on their seasonal migrations.

Their footprints (larger than my hand) can often be seen in the mud along the riverbank.

The trail farthest from the Stop River (as you head south on Causeway Street, it's the second trail with a green gate at the front) leads to one of the most secluded spots on the entire eighty-mile length of the Charles River. To reach the spot bear left at all intersections as you walk down the path. It is also possible to make a short loop through the reservation after viewing the river: Hike about halfway back up this path, past the first trail on the left, and take the second left onto another unmarked trail. It leads through pine, oak, and maple, then through a nice stand of beech. Go right at the end of this trail to return to Causeway Street.

This section of the Charles River has good bass and pickerel fishing. The canoeing is also good; in fact, it's easy to imagine you're paddling down the Amazon, rather than a suburban river.

Getting There

From Route 128, take Exit 16 onto Route 109 west. Go 7.7 miles, passing through Medfield Center. Turn left onto Causeway Street (just a couple hundred feet after crossing Route 27). Drive 1.8 miles on Causeway Street to the second green gate on the right. There is no formal parking, but you could pull off the side of the road or park at the small lot at nearby Noon Hill Reservation and walk back (only a half-mile).

Noon Hill Reservation
Medfield
204 acres

Recommended walk: 2 1/2 miles, 1 hour

There are a number of reasons why I visit heavily wooded Noon Hill over and over again, but its seclusion and diversity of wildlife are at the top of my list. Few people even know of its existence; as an added bonus it abuts the Henry L. Shattuck Reservation, which includes an additional 225 acres along the Charles River.

One bright March weekend afternoon I took a ramble to the top of Noon Hill and never saw another soul. But I did see wildlife. As I started my hike I decided to take a quick look at Holt Pond, which is adjacent to the small parking area. Circling above the pond was a huge black turkey vulture. The vulture's peaceful flight was quickly interrupted by the harassing action of a crow, which hounded the vulture so much it finally left the pond. The crow looked tiny next to the vulture's seven-foot wingspan, but crows do a good job diving and pecking larger birds such as vultures, owls, and hawks. Whenever you hear a bunch of crows cawing, have your binoculars ready—oftentimes they are harassing or "mobbing" a larger bird. It is said that crows are so smart that once

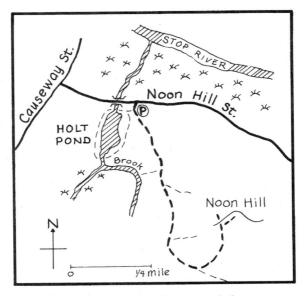

shot at, they soon learn to distinguish between people that are armed and those that are not.

After this aerial battle subsided I began my hike up the hill by taking the wide trail at the left of the pond next to the parking area. White-tailed-deer tracks were clearly visible in the two inches of snow that blanketed the ground. In the warmer months the same trail is carpeted with pine needles from the towering white pines that share this section of the forest with oaks, beech, birch, and a scattering of maples. The first part of the path is relatively flat and is lined on each side by gray, lichen-covered stone walls. Look for chipmunks and red squirrels running in and out of the rock openings in the wall.

As you continue on the trail you will pass through a low-lying area where a spur of the trail goes to the right. This is not the way to the top, but it is worth a side trip down this path as it leads you to a tiny mountain stream (Holt Brook) that tumbles over granite boulders as it makes its way down to Holt Pond. The path passes over the stream on a bridge made of overlapping stone. It's a fine spot for a rest and a snack. Over the years I have seen fox, ruffed grouse, and owls in this area. The ruffed grouse (called partridge by old New Englanders) stays with us through the winter and always gives me a start when I walk by one. (Thoreau wrote that "whichever side you walk in the woods the partridge bursts away on whirring wings," adding that "this brave bird is not to be scared by winter.")

Back on the main trail, you will soon come to another fork in the path; stay to the right to continue toward Noon Hill (do not go left through the stone wall). After ten or fifteen more minutes of hiking, covering about a half-mile, you will be at the base of the hill. Beech trees and exposed boulders hug the slopes to your left. A small path makes a direct assault on the hill but it's a steep and difficult climb. The main trail circles Noon Hill, allowing for a gentler climb. The trail splits again—stay to the left and you will soon be on the ridge of the hill. The best spot for viewing the countryside is an exposed rocky area that lies a few feet off the main trail to the right. The views from the crest look out toward the southeast where you can look down upon Medfield and Walpole in the foreground.

Noon Hill got its name from the early settlers who noted that the sun rose above the hill about noontime. It is said that King Philip (or Metacomet), the Native American leader of the Wampanoag tribe, launched his bloody raid on the town of Medfield from here. However, some historians say that on the day of the actual raid in 1676, the raiders were

Noon Hill Street passes through the maples and oaks at the base of the reservation.

amassed on the west side of the Charles River. No matter where the actual attack came from, this was probably an important area for the local Native Americans. They preferred to be situated near the confluence of major streams and rivers, and below Noon Hill the Stop River makes its entrance into the Charles River.

Noon Hill is owned by The Trustees of Reservations. Fishing is allowed on the pond and the trails are open for cross-country skiing (although they are hilly). There is a short, narrow trail around Holt Pond (a man-made pond, probably built around 1764 to power a sawmill). Look for kingfishers perched on branches above the pond.

Getting There

From Route 128, take Exit 16 onto Route 109 west. Follow it 7.7 miles (passing through Medfield Center). Turn left onto Causeway Street (just a couple hundred feet after crossing Route 27) and go 1.5 miles. Turn left again on Noon Hill Street. Drive 0.2 mile to a small parking area on the right.

Southwest of Boston

Stony Brook Nature Center and Wildlife Sanctuary
Norfolk
241 acres

Recommended walk: 1 mile, 30 minutes

Stony Brook Wildlife Sanctuary has a one-mile self-guided nature trail that offers excellent birdwatching opportunities and variety of terrain. Besides a long boardwalk through a marsh, the sanctuary has woods, rolling fields, ponds, a brook, and even a waterfall. It also has a nature center with exhibits and a garden with plants selected especially to attract butterflies.

The trail begins by the nature center building and heads west, bordered by a stone wall and surrounded by cedars, white birch, swamp maples, and black cherry. The trail is flat and wide, making this an excellent place for hiking with young children or anyone who has mobility limitations. In fact, the trail is navigable by wheelchair if an assistant is present to help over rough spots.

After an eight- to ten-minute walk, a long boardwalk takes you out over a marsh. If you lie down on

An old stone wall graces the path leading to the boardwalk at Teal Marsh and Kingfisher Pond, home to wood ducks, green herons, great blue herons, and Canada geese.

the boardwalk and look out over the edge, you might be able to see such underwater creatures as snapping turtles, sunfish, or insects swimming beneath the surface. The boardwalk leads to a small island covered with beech trees, where an observation deck offers a nice view of Kingfisher Pond. The pond is home to mallards, wood ducks, green herons, Canada geese, and black ducks. Look closely and maybe you will spot a great blue heron. These large birds are usually seen across the pond or perhaps in flight as they fly from one hunting spot to another.

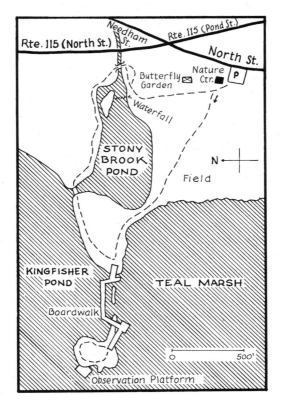

There is a great-blue-heron rookery near the property, but it has been wisely kept off-limits to the general public. The birds need an undisturbed area where they can raise their young. The nests, made primarily of twigs, are usually built at the tops of tall dead trees standing in a swamp. With the rookery situated near Kingfisher Pond, it's a good bet you can see one of these gray-colored birds as it silently stalks the pond's shoreline in search of small fish or frogs, which it snatches with its long bill.

Canada geese are scattered all about the property; they can be seen in the air, water, and in the fields. Some even spend the winter here rather than flying south. My three-year-old daughter and I hiked here in March, and she was mesmerized by the large geese that had gathered by the boardwalk.

After you have finished scanning the shoreline of Kingfisher Pond, recross the boardwalk and turn left at its beginning. You will soon walk over a bridge where the waters from Kingfisher Pond mingle with the smaller Stony Brook Pond. Be on the lookout for the shy and elusive wood ducks that make their nests in the specially erected boxes or in hollow trees. The babies emerge from the nest within twenty-four hours of birth and plummet onto the ground or into the water. With the ducklings so vulnerable because they cannot fly yet, the parents must be secretive in guarding their young. The best time to see wood ducks is in the fall, especially late in the day as they gather in small flocks, preparing for the migration southward. Besides the brilliant coloration of the male, a good method of identifying this species is by the large head, short neck, and long square tail.

The trail skirts the northern end of Stony Brook Pond and descends to where a clear flowing stream exits the pond. A path through the woods takes you down to the stream. At a small bridge across the stream, you can see the multileveled waterfall that

A red squirrel helps itself to the seed at Stony Brook.

spills out of Stony Brook Pond. Cascading water forms sheets of sparkling white spray. This is a beautiful spot; as you walk along the edge of the stream you can hear the splashing water ahead. Stone walls line the trail where red squirrels and chipmunks dart in and out of the boulders. At the edge of the falls a set of steps leads up from the stream and onto a meadow. It's hard to imagine that only sixty years ago this peaceful location was once the sight of a mill, producing first lumber and later textiles.

From the meadow you can see the nature center and the butterfly garden that mark the end of the hike. Be sure to take a few moments to rest by this garden. The plants were chosen for the nectar in the flowers, which the butterflies drink, or they are sources of food for caterpillars. If you decide to cultivate a butterfly garden, try growing some of the varieties of plants found here. Emily Brunkhurst, the former director of Stony Brook, recommends bee balm (a flower that attracts both butterflies and hummingbirds) and thistle. Emily also told me that "flowers that blossom at different times are also important." When a butterfly stops at a flower, grains of pollen cling to its body and then are rubbed off at the next one, thus pollinating the flowers, just as a bee does.

We usually think of butterflies as summer insects, but some of the best viewing at Stony Brook is in late September when monarch butterflies begin their migration southward. Other butterflies, such as the Baltimore butterfly, come out in early May and dazzle us with their black-and-orange coloring. As with the adults, each butterfly caterpillar looks quite different. The monarch caterpillar is yellow and gold, and you can sometimes spot them munching on such plants as milkweeds (another good plant to put in your butterfly garden).

Stony Brook can be a popular spot on weekends, but I would not term it crowded. For the best bird-watching come at dawn and bring your binoculars; April is an especially good month for birding, and the trails never get too muddy.

As with many Audubon sanctuaries, Stony Brook offers a variety of educational programs (including guided hikes for children) and volunteer opportunities for both children and adults. Occasionally, the sanctuary offers guided hikes into the swamp for adults to see the great-blue-heron rookery.

Getting There

From I-95 take Exit 7, Route 140 northwest. Proceed about 5 miles to Route 115 north (on right). Follow 115 for about 1.5 miles to intersection with Route 1A. Cross Route 1A and follow Route 115 north for another 1.5 miles to the third left, which is North Street. The sanctuary entrance is on the right. (Bristol Blake Reservation is part of Stony Brook Wildlife Sanctuary.) The sanctuary is open from dawn to 6:00 PM and is closed on Mondays in the winter. There is a slight admission fee if you are not a member of the Massachusetts Audubon Society.

Harold B. Clark Town Forest

Foxboro

300 acres

Recommended walk: 1 1/2 miles, 40 minutes

For wildlife and scenic beauty, town forest land usually can't compete with property owned by such groups as Audubon or The Trustees of Reservations. But the Harold B. Clark Town Forest is worth a visit because the main trail circles a secluded woodland pond. The shallow waters of Upper Dam Pond provide not only a visual diversity in the surrounding oak and pine forest, but the water also attracts such wildlife as raccoons, foxes, great blue herons and weasels that prowl the shoreline.

This hike is a short, forty-minute walk around the pond. The trail is wide and the terrain is primarily level, but cross-country skiers should be warned that it will take more than a couple of inches of snow to cover the large rocks and boulders protruding from the ground. Children find the hike to their liking because at the back end of the pond the trail passes close to the water's edge and they might see frogs, turtles, or perhaps a sunfish guarding its spawning bed in the late spring or early summer.

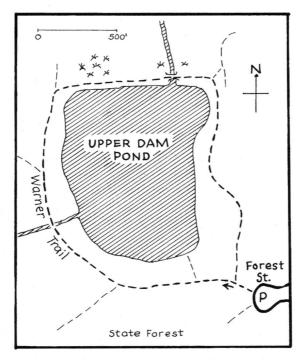

Begin your outing by parking at the end of Forest Street. Two trails lead into the woods: The trail on the left goes into F. Gilbert Hills State Forest and is marked by a sign saying "lookout rock." The trail described here is the one on the right with the sign welcoming you to Harold B. Clark Town Forest. (Harold B. Clark was one of the founders of the Foxboro Conservation Commission, and he played a large role in protecting the town's open space and wild areas.)

Proceed down the main trail and stay left at the first intersection just before the pond. This walk will take you in a clockwise loop around the blue-green waters of Upper Dam Pond. A few feet beyond this first intersection you will notice a spur off the main trail that leads to the water's edge. It's possible to drag a canoe from the parking area to this spot, but it's tough work. I canoed here once in the spring and caught a small bass and enjoyed watching the Canada geese paddle about. One goose was apparently on a nest, and when I got too close it lowered its neck and looked as if it might attack the canoe. I quickly backed up and gave it a wide berth.

The twenty-acre pond is relatively shallow, with many large boulders breaking the water's surface. Warm-water species such as largemouth bass and pickerel thrive in these types of ponds, but trout and smallmouth bass need deeper ponds where the water can stay cold, even in the summer.

Continuing on the main trail, you will soon reach an intersection where you should go right. (Always bear right after passing that first intersection and you will have no trouble circling the pond without getting lost.) The trail you are now on is part of the thirty-four-mile AMC Warner Trail, built and maintained by members of the Appalachian Mountain Club. Over the years I've hiked a good portion of the trail in such towns as Canton, Sharon, Foxboro, and Wrentham. It tends to follow rocky ridges and is strenuous to hike as well as difficult to follow in some places. The trail may not be perfect, but I love the concept—a wooded path running from suburban Canton, Massachusetts, all the way into Rhode Island.

As you begin to follow the southwestern end of the pond, you will pass over a tiny brook that rises out of a hillside swamp and spring, then tumbles down into the pond. During high-water periods, the brook makes quite a commotion as it drops over a series of

A spring-fed brook splashes down to Upper Dam Pond in the Harold B. Clark Town Forest.

boulders. You can explore the brook as it descends through an old stone wall and then into the pond.

At the north end of the pond take a right on a narrow trail that runs along the top of an earthen dam. Foxboro Conservation Manager David Risch told me that the pond was built approximately 160 years ago as a holding pond for a mill. Take a moment to marvel at the work that went into this earthen dam. In some places it is eight feet high, constructed from boulders, small stones, and dirt. What physical effort it must have taken to build such a work using only a team of oxen or horses! The same effort holds true for the miles of stone walls found throughout Massachusetts.

At the end of the earthen dam you should turn right to complete your loop of the pond. The trail climbs a ridge before bringing you back to the beginning of the circuit.

Risch also told me that there is a small herd of deer on the property. The white-tailed deer is a shy, elusive creature. Many of us believe that they only exist outside of Route 495, but, in fact, they are living in a number of suburban towns. They tend to stay close to swamps, both for safety and because wetlands and river corridors are often the only sizable areas left in their natural state.

Deer will come out of their secret bedding area at dusk to feed on grasses, twigs, buds, apples, corn, and acorns or seeds. Does will often travel in small herds, while mature bucks are solitary creatures for most of the year. During the fall rut, however, the bucks are quite active, following the scent of the does and doing battle with other bucks who invade their territory. In the winter, when the snow is deep, deer congregate in deeryards—areas protected from the chill of the winter's winds. I once came upon a deer-yard, located beneath large hemlocks; the sight of so many deer in a two-acre area was something I'll never forget.

Getting There

From I-95 take Exit 7 and follow the signs along Route 140 north to Foxboro. Go about 4 miles from the exit ramp (passing through Foxboro Center) and look for Lakeview Street on your left. Turn left on Lakeview Street and travel a half-mile to Forest Street on your right. Turn right onto Forest Street and park at its end (just 0.2 miles down). Remember to stay clear of the fire lanes that lead into the woods.

F. Gilbert Hills
State Forest
Wrentham/Foxboro
972 acres

Recommended walk: Blue Triangle Loop,
1 1/2 miles, 45 minutes

A number of rocky ridges, swamps, and secluded
ponds provide the hiker with diverse scenery at the
sprawling F. Gilbert Hills State Forest. The forest has
a wide assortment of such trees as red pine, spruce,
tupelo, and dogwood, as well as abundant wildlife
including deer, pheasant, grouse, and fox. The Civil-
ian Conservation Corps was active here during the
1930s, hacking out many of the roads, planting red
pines, and digging water holes to provide a ready
source of water in case of forest fire. Seventeen of
these stone-lined water holes can still be seen, with
most of them situated along High Rock Road.

There are miles of trails to explore, including a
portion of the thirty-four-mile AMC Warner Trail,
which runs from Canton, Massachusetts, to Cumberland, Rhode Island. The trail is dedicated to Charles
Henry Warner, who with fellow hiker John Hudson
conceived the idea of a woodland trail that linked the
Boston area to Rhode Island. At age eight-three Mr.
Warner actually walked twenty-five miles of the trail!

The best time to visit this state forest is on Sundays when hunting is not allowed. There is a short, 1.5-mile walk along the Blue Triangle Loop Trail that is a nice trail for first-time visitors or those walking with children. More ambitious hikers may want to make a larger loop (4.4 miles) on Acorn Trail to Warner Trail to High Rock Road. Just be sure to stay

The Blue Triangle Loop at F. Gilbert Hills State Forest is a good child-length walk.

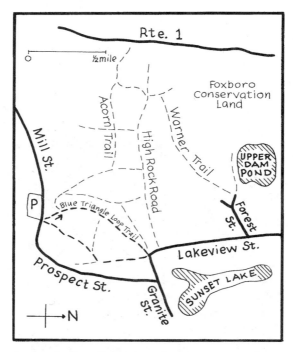

Rte. 1

½ mile

Foxboro
Conservation
Land

Acorn Trail

Mill St.

High Rock Road

Warner Trail

UPPER
DAM
POND

P

Blue Triangle Loop Trail

Forest St.

Lakeview St.

Prospect St.

Granite St.

SUNSET LAKE

N

on the marked trails as it's easy to get lost in a large
forest like this. There is a bulletin board outside the
public restrooms that has a map of the forest, rules
and regulations, and other information. A supply of
trail maps is also available there.

Our outing follows the Blue Triangle Loop Trail,
which is well marked with blue triangular signs. It
begins by heading from the parking lot through an
area of white pines and oaks, where a scattering of
spruce and large boulders add contrast to the forest.

The trail bears right where it narrows, and eventually passes by a crumbling stone wall, with its various shades of green moss mottled on the gray stone beneath. Just past the intersection with the stone wall is a muddy spot where two logs, cut lengthwise, act as a bridge to help keep your feet dry.

The trail soon intersects with Granite Street, where you walk right about fifteen feet before the blue triangles direct you back into the woods to the right. A bit of the Wolf Meadow Swamp can be seen on the right as the trail heads through a thick stand of hemlock. At the intersection of Pine Hill Trail, stay to the right, and then follow the blue markers that soon lead you to the left along a smaller, hilly trail that winds through pine trees. This trail brings you back to the parking lot after about a ten-minute walk.

Be on the lookout for ruffed grouse, which often stay perfectly still until you approach too closely, and then explode to air in rapid flight. Another bird you might see is the pheasant. Ring-necked pheasants were first introduced in the U.S. from Asia in 1881. They have a distinctive white ring around their necks, and their feathers have hues of green, purple, and red. There are few purebred pheasants left as the ring-necked and the English pheasant have been bred together extensively.

In the fall and winter pheasants congregate together, but in the spring the males go off to establish their harems, crowing regularly to attract the hens. The hens lay an average of twelve to thirteen eggs, and the male goes on its way, leaving all the parenting to the hen.

Owls also make their home at F. Gilbert Hills, probably preferring to roost in the thick cover of Wolf Meadow Swamp. The barred owl is a nocturnal predator with an incredible sense of hearing, able to detect the scurrying of mice as they forage along the forest floor. With a silent approach the owl can swoop through the woods, snatch a mouse, and then return to its perch as quietly as it approached.

I was surprised to read that Thoreau once caught an owl in his hands in broad daylight. He saw a screech owl from his boat, "landed two rods above, and, stealing quietly up behind the hemlock, though from the windward, I looked carefully around it, and, to my surprise, saw the owl still sitting there. So I sprang round quickly, with my arm outstretched, and caught it in my hand." It's rare to see an owl in the daytime, but on many camping trips I've awakened with a start to their eerie hooting.

Many of the other, longer trails are popular with mountain bikers and also provide a challenge for cross-country skiers due to the many hills.

Getting There

From I-95 take Exit 7 and follow Route 140 north about 1.7 miles to Foxboro Center. At Foxboro Center go almost all the way around the rotary and take South Street (which will be on your right after you go around the rotary) for a mile and a half, then turn right onto Mill Street. Go 0.5 mile on Mill Street to the entrance. Parking is across the street from the Forest Fire Station and the forest administration building.

Moose Hill Wildlife Sanctuary

Sharon
1,435 acres

Recommended walks: Bluff Head, $2^1/_2$ miles, $1^1/_2$–2 hours
Eastern Section: $1^3/_4$ miles, 1 hour.

Have you ever longed to find some secluded hilltop and just sit peacefully, letting the breeze and quietness lull your senses? I have, and Moose Hill Wildlife Sanctuary in Sharon has one of the best views in the region. The stunted cedar trees and the sheer rock walls give the illusion that this is a hilltop in Maine, New Hampshire, or Vermont. And for a view this good, the trail to the top is surprisingly gentle.

The sanctuary has varied topography, much of which was once farmland, now reverted back to forest. Over 400 species of wildflowers grow here, and due to the high elevations found in the sanctuary there are yellow and white birches to add to the feeling of being in the North Country. There are no moose here, but the origin of the sanctuary's name is from the moose that were said to inhabit the area in the late 1700s and early 1800s.

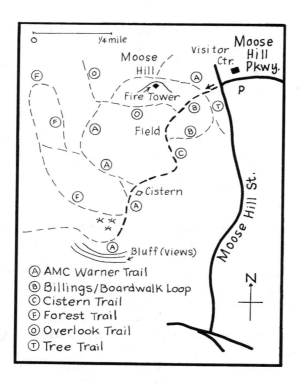

Scale: ¼ mile

Moose Hill

Moose Hill Pkwy.

Visitor Ctr.

Ⓐ

Fire Tower

Ⓞ

Field

Ⓑ

Ⓑ

Ⓣ

Ⓒ

P

Ⓕ

Ⓞ

Ⓕ

Ⓐ

Ⓕ

Ⓐ

Cistern

Ⓐ

Ⓐ Bluff (views)

Moose Hill St.

N

Ⓐ AMC Warner Trail
Ⓑ Billings/Boardwalk Loop
Ⓒ Cistern Trail
Ⓕ Forest Trail
Ⓞ Overlook Trail
Ⓣ Tree Trail

Bluff Head Walk

To begin your walk up to Bluff Head, cross Moose
Hill Street from the parking area and look for the
stone pillars that mark the entrance to the
Billings/Boardwalk Loop Trail (the stone pillars are
exactly opposite the intersection of Moose Hill Street
and Moose Hill Parkway). The trail follows a wide
grassy road that's easy on the legs. Mobility-

152   Southwest of Boston

impaired people can enjoy the first half-mile of this outing before the trail narrows and begins its ascent of the bluff. Stone walls and large sugar maples line the trail making it a visual treat. Stay on the Billings/Boardwalk Loop Trail as it curves to the left. Soon you will pass the old Billings barn on the left and two enormous maples on the right. Look for red and gray squirrels scrambling on their branches.

Exposed rocky cliffs and cedar trees can be seen at Bluff Head, which offers a tremendous view.

Other animals in the sanctuary include skunk, opossum, fox, raccoon, and deer. All are nocturnal, so your best bet at catching a glimpse of them is at dawn or dusk. The bird life is varied and easier to see. Some of the birds present are warblers, nuthatches, scarlet tanagers, northern orioles, bluebirds, woodpeckers, and a wide assortment of hawks such as kestrels, red-tailed hawks, and broad-winged hawks. (While sitting atop 600-foot Bluff Head during the autumn, you might be able to see a hawk riding a thermal on its migration.)

A short way down the Billings/Boardwalk Loop Trail is a circular opening in the woods where an assortment of trees are labeled, providing the perfect classroom for a young naturalist interested in identifying white pine, Colorado blue spruce, white birch, hickory, red oak, red pine, sassafras, and northern white cedar. After studying the trees, continue down the trail (look over your shoulder to see the blue spruce framed against the sky). Soon you enter another open area of low-lying plants and bushes; there are unusual species of wildflowers present at Moose Hill as well as twenty-seven species of ferns. Spring is the time to see the best show of colors.

The trail soon intersects with another; go right on Cistern Trail, marked with a C on a post. Here the hiking gets harder: Exposed roots on this narrow trail seem to grab at your boots. A maple, oak, and pine forest surrounds the trail. On the left you will pass a huge round cistern dug into the earth and lined with stones. The trail now becomes part of the AMC Warner Trail, which is a thirty-four-mile trail going from Canton, Massachusetts, to Diamond Hill in Cumberland, Rhode Island. Just beyond the cistern is an impressive stand of beech trees on the left and a swampy area on the right.

Here is where the trail starts its gradual climb to the bluff. But the designers of the trail knew what they were doing when they picked this route to the summit: it never gets steep and is a relatively easy walk to the top. Just as you begin your final steps to the summit you will see the gnarled and windswept branches of the eastern red cedars that dot the hilltop. These trees can be distinguished from the white cedars because of their needlelike leaves with bluish green berries. These hard fruits are eaten by birds.

The granite ledge at Bluff Head offers sweeping views to the south and west. Sullivan Stadium, home of the Patriots, can be seen just a few miles off. This is one of the nicest hilltops in eastern Massachusetts; it's the perfect place to sit, gaze off in the distance, and let your mind wander. No traffic sounds can be heard, only the breeze as it whispers through the cedars. There are a number of outcrops along this hilltop ridge with each one offering a change in the vista.

When you are ready to head home, retrace your steps back to the parking lot. The total hike takes between one and one-half and two hours, but allow extra time to rest at the bluff. More ambitious hikers can try the Forest Trail, which makes a long loop at the northern end of the property (see map).

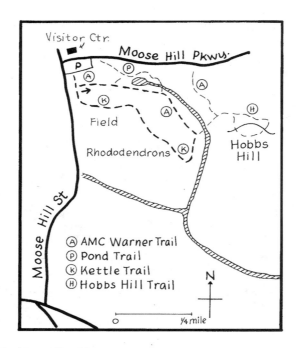

Eastern Section

On another trip, you may want to try the less-traveled eastern end of the property. Recently a coyote was seen on the property, and I think it's only a matter of time before another is spotted, especially in this secluded area of the sanctuary. A trail leaves the parking lot and follows Moose Hill Street southward a few feet and turns left (eastward) into the forest, first descending through an oak-pine woodland. (The trail is marked by an **A** on the map and is actually part of the Warner Trail.) After about a ten-minute walk the path follows a bubbling brook. Swamp maples soon mix in with the other trees as the trail veers to the southeast.

Some people prefer to go on to Hobbs Hill at the junction of the Warner, Hobbs Hill, and Kettle trails (see map), but I usually make a shorter outing to see the flowering shrubs along the Kettle Trail. The Kettle Trail will lead you back toward the parking lot. Turn right off the Warner Trail at the junction.

The Kettle Trail got its name for the many kettle hole depressions formed by huge blocks of ice left by the glaciers roughly 12,000 years ago. It is rugged in spots, hugging the ridges that are called eskers. The eskers formed when streams, flowing beneath the glacial ice sheets, deposited sediments along the stream bed that now make up the thin ridge line. Wildflowers abound here—pink lady's slippers, jack-in-the-pulpits, and maple leaf viburnum, to name just a few. But the highlight of this trip is the beautiful basin filled with mountain laurel and rhododendrons. If you happen to hike through here in early summer, you just might hit the peak of the bloom. Seeing plants with dazzling displays of color in a wild, natural setting is much more impressive to me than the same plants growing around the foundation of a home.

The trail continues back toward the parking lot, passing through a stand of hemlocks and then by a lush green field on the left. Making frequent stops, I usually complete the loop in an hour or an hour and fifteen minutes.

The sanctuary is open every day except Monday from 8:00 AM to 6:00 PM and a modest fee is charged for nonmembers of Massachusetts Audubon. Sanctuary programs range from children's programs to birdathons and guided field trips.

Getting There

Take Exit 10 off I-95 south, and take a left off the ramp. At the intersection, take a right onto Route 27 north toward Walpole. Follow Route 27 for 0.5 mile. Take a left onto Moose Hill Street and travel 1.5 miles uphill. Parking is on the left.

Take Exit 8 off I-95 north, and take a right off the exit ramp onto Main Street. Travel approximately 1 mile. Turn left onto Moose Hill Street and drive 1.5 miles; parking is on the right.

Borderland State Park
North Easton
1,570 acres

Recommended walk: 3 $1/2$ miles, 1 hour, 45 minutes

Hiking alongside water makes an outing special, and Borderland State Park has no fewer than six ponds to explore. Add to that the combination of flat hay fields or the option to test your legs on hilly, rocky terrain, and Borderland has something for everyone.

Wildlife also find Borderland to their liking; deer, fox, raccoon, and otter are just some of the mammals that live here. Park Supervisor Bob Babineau said that "it seems the deer are increasing—we see them in the fields in the early evening." He added that the park is a good place to view migratory birds: "Sometimes we even see osprey by the ponds." The ponds are shallow, but they hold such warm-water fish species as largemouth bass and pickerel.

Borderland was opened as a state park in 1971. Prior to that it served as the country estate of the Ames family, who named it Borderland because it is on the border of Sharon and Easton. The family constructed the stone mansion in 1910. It is open to visitors for regularly scheduled guided tours in the spring, summer, and fall.

Two large, plump Canada geese, identified by the black head and white check, feed on the grasses at Borderland.

Prior to the Ames family ownership, the ponds and streams powered a number of different mills in the eighteenth century and early nineteenth century. There was a sawmill, nail factory, cotton mill, and ironworks located here at various times. The nearby land was cleared for farming, and stone walls can still be seen crisscrossing the woodlands.

Small rocky hills cover the northern acres, while flatter land lies to the south. Some of the ponds are

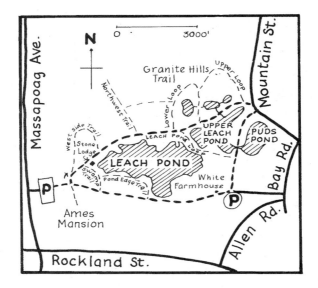

covered with water lilies and blue-flowered pickerel weed in the summer. All are shallow with significant amounts of vegetation growing, and when I canoed here with a friend we did as much pushing as paddling. (We heard the bass fishing was good, but we only caught one that evening.) As the vegetation dies and fills the bottom of the ponds, swamp shrubs begin to encroach along the shoreline, and the ponds will slowly turn to marsh.

It is possible to make either a 3-mile loop via the Leach Pond Loop or a 3.5-mile walk by continuing to make a circle around Upper Leach Pond. From the parking lot off Massapoag Avenue follow the gravel path through the fields (the mansion will be off to your right). At the T in the trail there is an excellent map posted. Go left here to start your walk on the north side of the ponds. (Follow the sign that says "Leach Pond.") The trail leads down to the water's edge where a stone building called the Lodge is located. (The pond-side trails are wide, flat, and well maintained, excellent for cross-country skiing.)

This is a good spot for viewing waterfowl. On my last visit, however, I spent a few minutes watching a red-tailed hawk circle the pond. It sent out a high scream as it scanned the grassy shoreline for rodents. The red-tailed hawk has adapted fairly well to man's presence; they can often be seen along our highways, perched in trees and keeping a sharp eye out for any movement in the grassy strips along the roadways. They are one of the few birds that winters here, and their hardiness was acknowledged by Thoreau when he wrote of "the hawk with warrior-like firmness abiding the blasts of winter."

Follow the trail to the left along Leach Pond, passing by the entrance to the West Side Trail (entering left). At various intervals are benches facing the water, offering scenic views of the islands near the pond's center. The woods along the trail are typical of southeastern Massachusetts, comprised primarily of oaks and white pines. Near the junction of the Northwest Trail you will see fields to the right that deer are said to frequent. Farther up the trail on the left is a little stone cave that was probably a farmer's root cellar.

Separating Leach Pond from Upper Leach Pond is Long Dam, built by the Ames family to create Leach Pond. If you wish to limit your walk to three

The wide fields at the southeast end of Borderland's Leach Pond are visited by deer at dusk.

miles, turn right here, cross the stream on the wooden footbridge and follow this path until its end, and then go right to reach the parking lot.

For the 3.5-mile loop continue following the pond-side trail to the northeast. There is an interesting unnamed side trail you might want to explore that runs off to the left through a field. It leads to a dike that separates two secluded ponds—a good place to spot wading birds such as the great blue heron. (On one occasion I continued on this trail, taking a path that forks to the right toward the Upper Loop Trail. The path follows a ridge that is quite rocky and steep, passing through an area where glacial boulders or erratics are strewn about.)

The pond-side trail takes you around Upper Leach Pond and eventually to the old Tisdale cellar hole, near Mountain Street, where there is a beautiful view of Upper Leach Pond. The trail intersects with Mountain Road, and you must follow this a few feet to the right before the path leads back into the woods at a gate on the right. This pathway soon takes you to a bridge that spans the outflow stream from Puds Pond.

Follow this trail all the way to the white farmhouse and bear right. The fields and wooden fence here are especially scenic, and I've taken some great photos facing back toward the farmhouse. The wide, level trail next passes by a large cove of Leach Pond (this is where I launched my canoe, parking in the small lot nearby). There are a few rare Atlantic white cedars growing adjacent to the cove, and Pond Edge Trail will be on your right. You can either take Pond Edge Trail, Swamp Trail, or the main trail back toward the parking lot and the Ames mansion.

On one of my hikes I returned back to the parking lot at dusk and saw an opossum scurry underneath my car. It was easily recognizable with its long, thin, hairless tail. With the aid of a flashlight I was able to get a close-up look at the creature. It had a grayish black coat of fur on its body and white fur on its face. Its dark, beady eyes and prominent pink nose stood in contrast to its light-colored facial fur. Usually the only opossums I see are dead ones in the road, but this little fellow was getting an early start to its evening of foraging, probably attracted to a discarded piece of food in the parking lot. They will eat just about anything found in the woods and swamps: meats, insects, plants, and fruits.

Borderland can be a popular place, but with 1,570 acres it's easy to find the quiet and solitude that makes hiking special. The park also offers organized hikes and birdwatching—call 508-238-6566.

Getting There

From I-95 take Exit 8 and follow South Main Street 3.5 miles to Sharon Center. Turn right on Billings Street at the traffic signal, then immediately right on Pond Street. Head south on Pond Street for 0.9 mile to a small rotary and continue on Massapoag Avenue. Drive 3.7 miles on Massapoag Avenue and the park entrance will be on the left.

Pratt Farm Conservation and Recreation Area
Middleborough
160 acres

Recommended walk: 1 ^{1}/$_2$ miles, 45 minutes

Trotting through beneath the tall white pines of Pratt Farm, the gray fox paused to see if I was following. Then, in a seemingly effortless motion, it leapt over a fallen tree and vanished into the underbrush. Surely foxes are the most handsome creatures of the forest.

A hiker always has the chance of seeing wildlife at Pratt Farm's fields, ponds, and forest. Located in the heart of cranberry country, Pratt Farm was spared from development in 1986 when the Middleborough Conservation Commission acquired the land for open-space preservation. With Middleborough's close proximity to Route 495, development pressures will likely continue, and the conservation work of far-sighted citizens will become even more important.

To begin your outing take the wide dirt trail that leads away from the parking area (there are two posts on either side of the trail's beginning). Picnic tables are scattered about in the sunny, open spots. On the left-hand side of the trail is a white pine and oak woodland, while on the right is former pastureland that is beginning its transformation back to for-

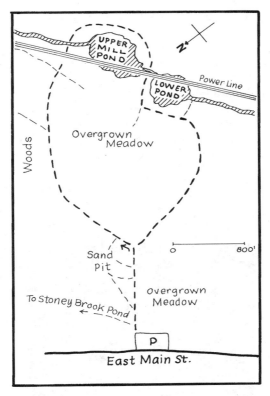

est. Red maples grow in the low-lying spots where the ground is moist, and cedar and pine are taking over the other areas of this overgrown meadow. As the forest matures, such hardwoods as oak and beech will establish themselves.

After about ten minutes into the walk, the main trail splits; go left and follow it through an open meadow. Look for cottontail rabbits under the staghorn sumac and other shrubs that provide them cover. Birds of prey are also attracted to such open areas as this where they can scan the field for any signs of movement. Fields like this would appeal to the American kestrel, which hunts from tree limbs or fence posts. These small but deadly "feathered bullets" will hunt insects and small rodents; once I even saw one bring down a blackbird.

The overgrown pastures at Pratt Farm attract fox, deer, skunk, and a variety of birds.

Continue following the trail as it hugs the edge of the field and passes beneath a power line (do not take the trail to the left that follows the power line). Just beyond the power line the path enters the low-lying woods and passes over a small stream. Large square-shaped stones can be seen lining the stream bed on the right-hand side of the trail, apparently the work of early farmers or mill owners.

Before the early settlers arrived this land was within the tribal boundaries of the Wampanoag Native Americans. It was the Wampanoags, under the leadership of Massasoit, who helped the Pilgrims survive their first years in the New World. They taught the settlers how to fish, hunt, and grow corn. This friendship was later strained as more and more English arrived and settlements expanded westward from Plymouth and Boston. By 1675 the Wampanoags had been displaced from much of their coastal lands. Fearing that they would soon lose their remaining land, the Wampanoags began the uprising known as King Philip's War. (The first attack occurred in nearby Swansea.) Ironically, the leader of the rebellion was Massasoit's son, Metacomet (named King Philip by the whites). The war was bloody and brief; it broke the power of New England's tribes.

Back on the trail, follow the path across the stream where it narrows and is blanketed with pine needles. Through the trees on your right you can see Upper Mill Pond, and you may hear ducks give a series of quacks as they notice your approach. The pond is small and shallow, but water always attracts wildlife. Look for the tracks of deer, raccoon, and fox.

It was on the far side of the pond that I saw the gray fox mentioned earlier. The gray fox is smaller than the red fox and is a skillful tree climber. They usually hunt in thick woods and eat a wide variety of small mammals, supplemented by insects, snakes, turtles, frogs, apples, and berries. It is said that they follow regular routes, following waterways and valleys on their hunting forays.

The trail circles behind the pond on a low hill. At one time a gristmill stood by the pond, and later an ice house and a trout hatchery. Through the woods on the left you can see a crumbling stone wall and on the right will be a large pine tree that somehow escaped the farmer's saw. On my last outing here I almost stepped in a fresh animal hole smack in the middle of the trail. It was probably built by a groundhog, but next to the hole was a yellow jackets' nest, which made me wonder if perhaps a skunk or raccoon had been digging there (both animals tolerate bee stings to get at nests for food). The inhabitant of the burrow did not show himself, but a few feet farther on a mouse ran out ahead of me—it too had built the entrance to its home right on the path.

Soon the path passes onto a neck of land between Upper Mill Pond on the right and the even smaller Lower Mill Pond on the left (the path is crowded by tree branches here). After crossing between the two, go left and visit the little bridge where the water exits the pond. This is a good spot for children to sit and observe the pond life.

From the bridge, retrace your steps a few feet and follow the path that bears to the left, up a small hill and into an open field. I stopped to rest in the meadow and while munching on an apple I heard crows cawing angrily in the distance. Whenever you hear crows making a racket, have your binoculars ready—this often means they are harassing a hawk or an owl. Sure enough, two minutes later a red-tailed hawk flew by, followed closely by two crows.

To return to the parking area simply continue straight on this path. It connects with the main trail, completing the loop around the ponds and fields. Turn left at the intersection to return to the parking lot. Total outing is a short and easy forty-five-minute walk.

If you are in this area in the winter consult a map to find Long Point Road on the Middleborough/Lakeville line, just south of Assawompset Pond and on the northern end of Great Quittacas Pond. Although these reservoirs are off-limits to the public, you can drive out on Long Point Road and scan the water for bald eagles, which are sometimes seen out on the frozen ponds.

Getting There

Pratt Farm is located on Route 105 (East Main Street) in Middleborough, near the Nemasket River. From Route 495 take Exit 6 and drive east on Route 44 about four and a half miles to its junction with Route 105. Turn south on Route 105, drive about 1.1 miles, and look for a sign on the left that welcomes you to the conservation land.

Cranberry Pond Conservation Area

Holbrook/Braintree
192 acres

Recommended walk: 2 miles, 1 hour

Within the heart of suburbia lie acres of hilly, rocky woodlands surrounding secluded little Cranberry Pond. The region of our walk is known as the Cranberry Pond Conservation Area, which is part of the Holbrook and Braintree town forests. For skunk, raccoon, and rabbit live in these woodlands. The diverse features here include exposed bedrock and scattered boulders (always fun for youngsters who enjoy climbing), a tiny rare quaking bog (complete with insect-eating sundews and pitcher plants), and a small stream that tumbles over rocks and boulders. In the spring and summer you will find wildflowers scattered through the forest of hemlock, beech, maple, and a scattering of shining holly trees that sparkle in the sun.

To begin your hike follow the trail at the end of Park Drive a short distance to where it intersects with the Wiggins Trail. Go left. The path is rather rough, but it's worth the effort. If you go in the autumn the foliage display is brilliant. There are a number of beech trees with yellow and gold leaves on their

A red fox kit soaks up the sun. The woodlands around Cranberry Pond are home to fox, skunk, raccoon, and many species of birds. (Paul Rezendes photo)

branches and their smooth gray trunks rise like granite columns. The scene is completed by fallen brown leaves carpeting the ground.

By following this trail you will reach a set of power lines, where you turn right for a few feet (staying beneath the power lines) and then turn left, where the trail heads back into the woods. You soon come to an enchanting little spot alongside a small brook. In dry periods the stream is no more than a trickle, but in wet weather it can really work up a head of steam as it cascades over the many rocks. A large boulder rests in the middle of the stream bed and water tumbles down around both sides. It's always nice to sit for a moment and listen to the relaxing sound of falling water.

Instead of crossing the stream, follow the trail to the right, where there are blue-painted blazes on the trees. A few minutes down the path you may want to

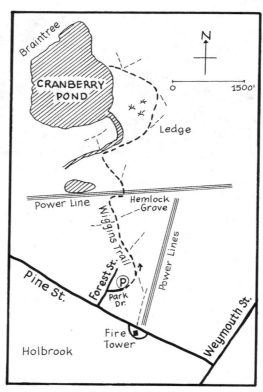

explore a large open ridge of exposed bedrock, off the trail to the right. The trail to Cranberry Pond passes in front of this ridge and descends a steep slope. On one walk, I noticed the October air was decidedly cooler and damper here, smelling more pungent and earthy. Through the bushes on the left is the tiny bog, with its unique vegetation. Thoreau loved such places, writing, "I enter a swamp as a sacred place, a sanctum sanctorum. There is the strength, the marrow of Nature."

The trail climbs again, and on the left is another area of exposed rock, with partial views of the pond below. From here you can walk down to the edge of the pond itself. It's a good place for seeing waterfowl and birds. On one visit, however, I had the misfortune of having a skunk cross my path when I was leaving the pond. It was just before dusk and the skunk was moving along the path at what seemed like an incredibly slow pace. Not taking any chances, I waited where I was for ten minutes and then resumed my walk, well aware of its lingering odor.

Skunks emerge at night to feed on grubs and other insects (they often make holes in suburban yards while digging for grubs). Surprisingly, they also feed on mice and even rabbits if they stumble upon a young one. The skunk has two large glands located at its rear that discharge a foul odor when it is threatened. It will usually give a warning by hissing, growling, or clicking its teeth, but once it fires it can hit a target up to twelve feet away. Don't get caught in a position where you see the skunk's tail come up—it might be too late.

The pond marks the end of this walk, which takes about an hour round-trip. On your way back you might want to turn left when you reach the power lines and go a short distance to see an area called "hemlock grove," visible just a few hundred feet down on the right.

There are many more trails with other entrances on the Braintree side of the town forest. For more information call the Braintree Conservation Commission at 617-848-1870.

Getting There

From Route 24, exit onto Route 139 east. Go 2 miles until you come to a T intersection at a stoplight. Turn right, continuing on Route 139 toward Holbrook. Go 2.7 miles and turn left on Weymouth Street. Go 0.5 mile and then turn left on Pine Street at the blinking light. Proceed 0.2 mile on Pine Street and then turn right on Forest Street. A few feet down, turn right on Park Drive. Park at the end of Park Drive and the entrance is directly ahead.

South of Boston

World's End Reservation
Hingham
251 acres

Recommended walk: 4 1/2 miles, 3 hours

World's End; what a great name. And what a great place. Should a visitor to eastern Massachusetts only have time to visit one natural area, I would recommend World's End. In my opinion this is the most beautiful reservation in the area and certainly one of the most scenic in the entire country.

With a glowing description like that, one might ask what makes this area so unique. First of all, World's End is a peninsula that juts out from the mainland separating Hingham Harbor from the mouth of the Weir River, providing magnificent views in every direction. (It is unknown who named World's End or why, but I assume it got its name because it is a peninsula.) The rolling, open terrain will make you feel like you're on the landscaped grounds of some English estate. Best of all, World's End is a prime spot for viewing migratory birds.

On my last visit to the reservation—a sunny May afternoon—I had no sooner parked my car than I spotted a black-capped night heron in the little marsh

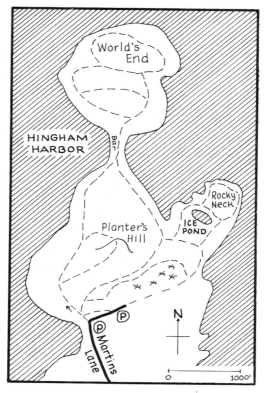

located just behind the ranger's office. Park Ranger Connie Mahoney was on duty and I asked him what other birds had been spotted recently. He pointed behind me, directing my attention to a larger section of the marsh where a beautiful white swan could be seen. It was a mute swan that had built its nest at the far end of the marsh. Mute swans are an Old World species that had been introduced into eastern North America and are now breeding in the wild.

Mahoney told me he had also seen cormorants, great blue herons, snowy egrets, quails, marsh hawks, kestrels, and of course the usual red-tailed hawks that love to hunt in such open areas as World's End.

The animal life included all the regular small mammals of New England, including the red fox. Mahoney described how a fox would make an early morning foray out of the reservation to investigate a clump of tall trees nearby. It seems the fox knew that crows were nesting in the trees and was checking the ground to see if any nestlings had fallen out. Another reason foxes are known as smart or sly is that they are extremely suspicious animals who rely on their strong sense of smell to avoid man. Yet they have learned to live in close proximity to man by making nocturnal forays to hunt for mice, moles, and other small rodents. The red fox can now be found all over North America, except for several western states (Washington, Oregon, California, Nevada, Arizona, and New Mexico).

Upon entering the reservation I took the trail to the left, which leads to the reservation's two smooth hills, geologically known as drumlins—elongated mounds created by the glaciers. When the last glaciers began to retreat 15,000 years ago, their action ground the bedrock beneath them into gravel, silt, and clay, which was then deposited into the egg-shaped drumlins. Drumlins are usually less than a mile in length and much smaller than our high bedrock ridges and mountains.

The paths leading through the open meadows were designed by famed landscape architect Frederick Law Olmsted in 1890 as part of a proposed development, which fortunately never came to be. However, the winding roads and the stately rows of trees that line them are here for all to enjoy. Prior to Olmsted's plan the area had been stripped for timber and only three elm trees remained on all of World's End. The tree-planting program that followed Olmsted's plan transformed the bare drumlins into a diverse landscape with a wide variety of trees, including imported English oaks.

Since that proposed planned community, World's End has escaped development a number of times. The property was considered for projects ranging from the site of a nuclear generator to development of public housing. It was even considered as a site for the United Nations! In 1967 the local citizens raised the necessary money for The Trustees of Reservations to purchase the property.

Today the trees that line the curving paths are quite large and contrast with the open fields on either side. Just a short way up the path is a sweeping view of Boston Harbor with the skyline of the city of Boston rising in the distance. The path then climbs Planter's Hill, which at 120 feet is the highest point on the reservation. Along the way there is an occasional bench placed at some of the more strategic points for capturing the magnificent views. On my walk here the red-tailed hawks Ranger Mahoney told me about were clearly visible, soaring above the top of Planter's Hill. Small clumps of woodlands, primar-

A curving, tree-lined path leads out to the edge of the World's End peninsula.

ily comprised of eastern red cedar and such tall hard-woods as maple and oak, provide habitat for a variety of small animals the hawks were hunting. Lichen-covered stone walls are visible in some spots, reminding you of the area's former agricultural days. Also visible along the woods and in the meadows is poison ivy—learn to recognize the plant's three-leaf stems and give it a wide berth.

After climbing the top of Planter's Hill to a tremendous viewpoint, the trail begins its descent to the sandbar that links the Planter's Hill drumlin to the main World's End drumlin. Early settlers built this causeway, known as the "bar," to allow travel between the two islands during high tide. (World's End reminds me of a miniature Boston before the Back Bay was filled. Prior to the mid-1800s, Boston was a peninsula connected to the mainland by a long "neck" or causeway, and I imagine it must have looked something like World's End.)

Crossing the causeway allows you easy access to the rocky beach; it's a perfect spot for children to go exploring. As you climb the outer hill look back toward Planter's Hill and admire the unique topography. Bring your camera—this is the kind of place you will want to capture on film. The outer island has two connecting roads that loop around this island's two highest mounds.

After exploring this area, cross the sandy causeway again, then bear left onto a road that leads to Rocky Neck. Through the trees on the left you can see the jagged cliffs of Rocky Neck, which stand in contrast to the smooth hills you have just explored. Many people bypass Rocky Neck, but in my opinion this is the best area on the whole peninsula.

Bear left at the next fork in the trail and then take the first left after that. As you enter Rocky Neck the open landscape changes to a more intimate area of woods where the trail is often shaded. You will soon come to the edge of a cliff that rises fifty feet above the water. This makes a fine place to sit and rest. I sat on this granite outcrop for quite awhile, taking in the smell of the ocean on the breeze. The sense of smell can enhance any hike—we should not let vision be the only means of enjoying nature.

Whenever I travel along the cool dark trails of Rocky Neck I rarely see another person, and this trip was no exception. Two cottontails, however, shared the same path just up ahead, but as usual, they would not stay still long enough to have their picture taken. These rabbits thrive in this combination of fields, shrubs, and small patches of woods. They were once much more common in New England when farmlands, rather than forests and developed areas, dominated the region.

On the right-hand side of the trail lies the Ice Pond, which seems quite out of place on this rocky point. The Ice Pond was built in 1909 by farmers as a nearby source to cut ice in the winter. Today, the pond attracts wildlife: A mallard took wing as I approached. The mallard is a common and wide-ranging fowl that often flocks with black ducks. They are surface feeders that eat aquatic vegetation and an occasional insect or mollusk. The males have green heads with white neck bands and rusty breasts. Females are a mottled brown, and both sexes have a distinctive blue rectangle at the hind area of their wings. When you surprise a mallard it often lets out a loud quack and takes off nearly vertically.

This little pond adds to the enchanting character of Rocky Neck. And if it's springtime, flowering trees, such as the apple tree (whose blossoms have such a sweet smell), will be in bloom. Every season is a good one at World's End; in the summer there are often cool ocean breezes, in the fall the foliage is alive with color, and in the winter the cross-country skiing is superb when there is enough snow to cover the gentle slopes. Sea ducks are also seen more frequently in the winter.

After walking the perimeter of Rocky Neck the trail you are on soon intersects with another. I usually turn left here and pass by the northeastern end of the marsh. Just as you reach an area of hemlock trees on a knoll (about a quarter-mile down the path),

Mute swans were introduced to North America from Europe and now breed in the wild.

there is a trail going through a field on the right—
this leads to the boardwalk that passes through tall
cattails and marsh grass. You can hear the birds in
the reeds but it's impossible to see them. However,
just up ahead is a rock ledge that offers a sweeping
view of the marsh. The ledge can easily be climbed
from the rear, and it's a great place to sit and watch a
few minutes of marsh life unfold.

From here it's only a short walk to the parking
lot by continuing on this foot trail or by returning to
the cart path by the hemlocks and going right (southwest). The whole walk took me about three hours, so
you may want to carry some drinking water. I estimate I walked about four and a half miles.

World's End is not a secret spot, and on warm
weekend afternoons the parking lot can fill up. There
is a slight admission charge if you are not a member
of The Trustees of Reservations. Picnicking and
swimming are not permitted.

Getting There

From Route 3 take Exit 14 to Route 228 north. Go 6.6
miles to Route 3A and turn left. Proceed on 3A for 0.9
mile, then take a right on Summer Street and proceed
for 0.3 mile. Cross Rockland Street at the light and
follow Martins Lane 0.7 mile to the entrance and
parking area.

Albert F. Norris Reservation

Norwell

117 acres

Recommended walk: 2 miles, 1 hour

Tom Foster, district supervisor for The Trustees of Reservations, referred to the Norris Reservation as a "jewel." He's right; the trails lead from heavily forested land to the banks of the historic North River, an estuarial river that winds its way through an incredibly scenic salt marsh.

From the parking lot a wide, well-groomed trail passes a small millpond where a gristmill and sawmill were built in 1690. Canada geese are often seen paddling about the shallow pond. Second Herring Brook exits the pond on the right and there are comfortable benches situated by both the side of the brook and the pond itself.

In 1992 a new trail was added to the reservation. It forks to the left just after the millpond and soon joins an old woods road that leads down to the river where there is an old, but well-kept, boat house. The trail is about a half-mile long.

I still prefer the original trail which forms a loop, first leading from the millpond and paralleling Second Herring Brook. Where the trail forks, stay to the right. It passes beneath large white pines, maples,

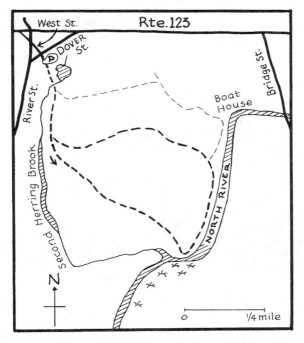

oaks, and a scattering of beech. Beneath these larger trees lies the American holly, a smaller understory tree. It can often be spotted by looking for its shiny leaves that twinkle in the sunshine. The holly is a deciduous evergreen that grows to about thirty feet in height. The South Shore of greater Boston marks the northernmost limit of its range.

After about a mile hike down the trail, you will catch a glimpse of the sparkling blue waters of the North River through the trees on your right. Soon

A short walk leads to the salt marsh on the North River where harrier hawks do their hunting.

you will come to an opening by the marsh where a bench has been strategically placed for resting by the river. It is especially beautiful here in the early morning, when you have the reservation all to yourself. While you sit in the shade, the sun illuminates the greens and golds of the marsh, providing the perfect frame for the blue river. The North River is a tidal waterway, and this mix of fresh and salt water produces a unique habitat attractive to a wide variety of waterfowl and shore birds. Anadromous fish, such as shad, migrate up the river each spring to spawn. The birds and animals seen here include marsh hawks, great blue herons, green herons, red fox, and mink.

Between 1645 and 1871 there were over two dozen shipyards located on the North River. One such site, Rogers Shipyard, was located not too far from the shores of Norris Reservation, on the opposite side of the river. Timber was stripped from all the surrounding towns to be used in the construction of the vessels. (Rogers Shipyard site can be visited by driving down Corn Hill Lane in Marshfield.)

The trail follows along the edge of the marsh. There are two more scenic openings, each with its own bench. When the tide is bringing in salt water, you can smell the sea in the air. Rapid tidal flows can make the river dangerous for canoeists, especially east of this area.

After this last river overlook the trail leads back through the woods (passing the new trail, mentioned earlier, on the right) and reconnects at the fork just below the millpond, completing the loop. From here it is only a five-minute walk back to the parking lot. The total walk takes about an hour and it is a great place to bring the kids.

Getting There

From the intersection of Routes 3 and 53 (Exit 13), take Route 53 north 0.6 mile, then turn right onto Route 123. Follow Route 123 for 3 miles. Take a right on West Street and drive 0.3 mile to its end.

Black Pond Nature Preserve
Norwell
120 acres

Recommended walk: 1 mile, 30 minutes

Black Pond is a quaking cedar bog with a variety of unique plants and trees. The trail is a short one, but within a forty-minute walk you can see three environments: a mature upland forest, a swamp forest, and the relatively rare sphagnum bog with one-acre Black Pond at its center. The plant life around the bog is so unusual that it gives one the feeling of being in a strange country.

To begin your walk, take the trail that starts by the welcoming sign; follow it about 100 feet until you reach a small clearing. The trail continues at the back end of this tiny meadow, where it enters the forest. I liked these woods the moment I entered them, because, rather than the usual oaks and pines so common in eastern Massachusetts, here the dominant trees are beeches, hemlocks, and American hollies. On a summer walk I took here in July, the temperatures were expected to reach the midnineties that day, so I started my outing at seven in the morning while the air was still cool beneath the canopy of towering trees.

About 250 feet from the meadow this trail meets a path that enters from the right. Turn right here—this is the way to the bog. Soon the moisture on the forest

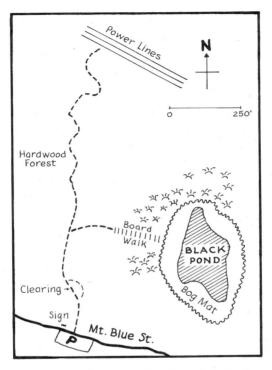

floor increases and you reach a boardwalk above the swamp. Strange plants, including large ferns, can be seen as bird calls echo through the woods. The setting gives one the feeling of being in a jungle.

Some of the rare plants found here include leatherleaf shrubs, rose pogonia, and bog orchids. The bog also has two insect-eating plants: the pitcher plant and the sundew. The pitcher plant attracts insects with the fluids that collect in its hollow leaves. The tiny hairs on the leaves allow the insects to enter, but the same hairs block their escape. The insects drown in the fluid and are digested in part by the plant's enzymes and in part by bacterial activity. The plant then absorbs the nutrients from the insects. You can spot the pitcher plant by looking for a plant roughly eight to twenty-four inches tall with a hanging red flower growing from the center of green or purplish pitcher-shaped leaves.

The sundew is much smaller and harder to find than the pitcher plant. It has round leaves with white or pink flowers growing just inches off the ground. It too traps insects in a sticky fluid, only this plant's leaves actually close upon the insect, trapping it in the fluid. The insects provide the plants with some of the nutrients, such as nitrogen, that are lacking in the bog.

As you walk closer to the pond, tall Atlantic white cedar trees begin to appear. The trees thrive in the soggy soil—I've never seen cedar trees so large. White cedar resist water decay, and for that reason they were extensively logged for such products as shingles, wooden gutters, piers, fence posts, and small boats.

After you pass the cedars, the pond will appear. It is ringed by a floating mat primarily comprised of sphagnum moss. (Because of the ability of sphagnum moss to absorb water, Native Americans used it for babies' diapers.) Bogs have little oxygen and nutrients, and many of the plants and aquatic life found in most ponds cannot survive here. Sphagnum moss, however, grows so well in these sterile environs that someday it will engulf the open water, allowing larger plant life, such as the white cedar, to fill the bog. It is estimated that there will be no open water left in another few hundred years.

The boardwalk extends to the right of the pond where it soon ends. Should you be interested in seeing more of the hemlock and beech forest, retrace your steps back to where the path to the pond left the main trail, and instead of heading left to the parking area, go to the right. This trail extends a few hundred

The boardwalk passes through ferns and Atlantic white cedar trees before reaching the quaking bog.

yards until it ends at a set of power lines. Some of the creatures that live here include fox, raccoon, skunk, ruffed grouse, and woodpeckers.

As you head back to Mt. Blue Street, note the inscription on the boulder in the little clearing. The bog was dedicated to William Vinal, who worked so hard to preserve this area. The dedication and inscription read: "Black Pond Preserve, A Class Room to Learn About the Unity of Life."

Getting There

Black Pond is operated by the Massachusetts Audubon Society for The Nature Conservancy. Visitors must gain permission before entering the property. Write or call the Massachusetts Audubon Society, 2000 Main Street, Marshfield, MA 02050; 617-837-9400.

From the Boston area take Route 3 south to Exit 13 (Route 53, Norwell). When you get off the exit take Route 53 north (left off exit ramp) for half a mile, then turn right onto Route 123 east. Follow Route 123 for about 3 miles, then turn left on Central Street. Go about 1 mile, then take a right onto Old Oaken Bucket Road. Stay on Old Oaken Bucket Road for 0.3 mile, then turn left onto Mt. Blue Street. Go about 0.7 mile. There will be a small parking area on the left (this is usually chained closed, so you will have to park on the street). Tucked in by the vines on the right-hand side of the road, opposite the parking area, is a small brown sign that says Black Pond. Drive slowly—it is easy to miss this entrance.

Daniel Webster
Wildlife Sanctuary
Marshfield
472 acres

Recommended walk: 1¹/₂ miles, 45 minutes

Over 300 acres of grasslands and 100 acres of mixed woodlands and water attract migratory birds and waterfowl to beautiful Daniel Webster Wildlife Sanctuary. This coastal property is also home to opossum, raccoon, mink, red fox, coyote, and weasel. The open area around the trails provides excellent long-range viewing, so bring your binoculars. You may have the good fortune to spot a northern harrier hovering over the marsh or, on rare occasions, a falcon.

These low-lying acres were once part of Daniel Webster's estate. On the north side of the sanctuary lies the Green Harbor River; on the south is Wharf Creek. For some reason this sanctuary receives fewer vistors than I would expect, perhaps because there are other Audubon properties and extensive conservation areas nearby. On weekend mornings in the fall I have had the place all to myself. Spring, however, is the time to visit, when bird life is even more active.

The terrain here is open and flat—even Fox Hill is no more than a bump. The round-trip walk to Fox Hill via Fox Hill Trail and returning on Webster

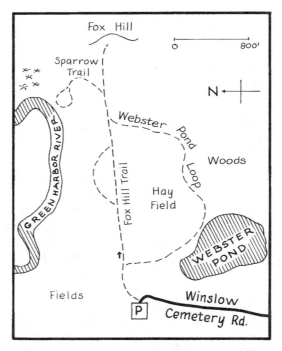

Pond Loop is a pleasant, nonstrenuous 1.5-mile stroll. From the parking area follow Fox Hill Trail as it leads through the open field toward Fox Hill. A small bench awaits you at the top of the hill where you can sit and watch the bird life come and go from the marsh. In the distance is a pole with an osprey nest built on its platform. On one of my visits the osprey was quietly perched on the edge of the nest.

The osprey first nested here in 1989, and one nestling was successfully hatched. In the second year three young were hatched and raised. But in the third year a predator took the eggs or nestlings. Maybe a raccoon climbed the pole and raided the nest.

The osprey is an uncommon bird in New England. The nest at Daniel Webster Wildlife Sanctuary was the first successful osprey nest known to be in this area in

Osprey can sometimes be seen circling above the marsh at Daniel Webster Wildlife Sanctuary. The osprey nest at the sanctuary was the first successful nest known to be in this area in over 100 years.

over 100 years. The banning of DDT has played a large role in the comeback of the osprey, but coastal development will probably keep their numbers low.

Osprey can be identified in flight by the crook in their long wings and the black wrist mark. Their overall coloring is brown above and white below. They are fish eaters, which they catch in their talons as they plunge feet first into the water. Their habitat is lakes, rivers, and the seacoast. Although they are not numerous around our waterways, osprey are seen during the spring and fall migrations. They winter from the Gulf Coast and California south to Argentina.

At the base of Fox Hill is a seasonal trail (open only in the fall) called Sparrow Trail, which brings you closer to the Green Harbor River before it forms a loop and reconnects. You can reach the Sparrow Trail by exiting Fox Hill the way you came up and turning right at the base of the hill. After you explore this area, take the Fox Hill Trail a few feet back toward the parking area and then turn left onto Webster Pond Loop. This trail hugs the edge of the field and woodlands before it reaches the vicinity of the pond where it turns left at a fence. It's a pleasant walk here with cedars and red maples lining the grassy path. You may not spot any unusual birds or any large birds of prey, but you can almost always find chickadees, titmice, mockingbirds, and bluejays.

At the pond you are likely to see Canada geese, even in the winter. More and more geese are staying in Massachusetts year-round. It is theorized they might be staying due to milder winters and more open fields to feed on. There is a bench at a vantage point above the pond, and this is a good place to soak up the solitude of the marsh before heading home.

Massachusetts Audubon is constructing bird observation blinds in the sanctuary and another trail off the Webster Pond Loop.

Getting There

From Route 3 south take Route 139 (Exit 12) east into Marshfield. Drive 3.8 miles and look for Webster Street on the right. (Webster Street is just 0.3 mile beyond the Route 3A intersection.) Proceed down Webster Street 1.7 miles and then go left on Winslow Cemetery Road. The sanctuary is at the end of Winslow Cemetery Road, about 0.75 mile.

North Hill Marsh Wildlife Sanctuary

Duxbury

137 acres

Recommended walk: 3 1/2 miles, 1 hour and 35 minutes

The locals that regularly visit North Hill Marsh tell me that the large fresh water pond here attracts all sorts of birds and waterfowl such as ring-necked and black ducks, mute swans, buffleheads, hooded mergansers, herons, kingfishers, and egrets. Wood ducks find this a good place to nest because of the dead timber standing in the pond and the many nesting boxes that have been erected. Recently, there have been a number of sightings of osprey near the pond, and a nesting platform has been erected to induce the osprey to nest here.

If you come with young children I recommend limiting your walk to the Yellow Loop Trail, which is about a mile in length and is clearly marked by yellow markings on trees. The trail starts at the parking lot and leads to the south shore of the pond before turning back to Mayflower Street, just a short distance from where you parked your car.

There are several miles of secluded (and confusing) nature trails, split between the east and west sides

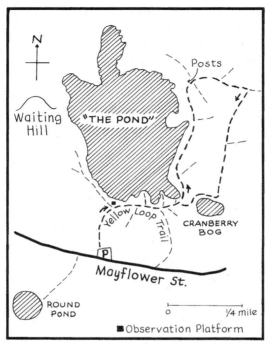

Waiting Hill

"THE POND"

Posts

CRANBERRY BOG

Yellow Loop Trail

P

Mayflower St.

ROUND POND

0   ¼ mile

■ Observation Platform

of the pond. Trails on the west side will take you to a small hill called Waiting Hill, which supposedly got its name when the wives of fishermen and merchants would look off the hill and scan the ocean for returning ships. (Today the woods obstruct the views.)

Our walk is on the east side of the pond, where we follow the trails that make a wide loop of the area. The first part of the outing hugs the pond's shoreline, and the return portion passes through a pine-oak forest and then goes on to a scenic cranberry bog.

Start your walk from the signboard at the parking lot and follow the Yellow Loop Trail down to the pond. An observation platform has been erected near the water, so bring your binoculars to scan the pond. The deadwood standing in the pond offers nesting birds a bit of protection from raccoons. (The man-made boxes with the small holes are for tree swallows and the boxes with larger holes are for wood ducks.) The timber is also excellent cover for such warm-water fish species as pickerel and largemouth bass.

The woods here are home to great horned owls. They do their hunting at night but sometimes people spot them perched on a limb of a tall white pine. If you are lucky enough to see one it's a sight you won't forget. I still recall the time I saw nesting great horned owls when I was nine years old and how shocked I was by the enormity of their size. They would swoop, ghostlike, into their nests, bringing mice, squirrels, rabbits, and skunks to their young.

From the observation platform follow the yellow markings on the hilly trail. You will pass a trail to the right marked by red discs, followed by a trail to the left that ends at the pond's edge. A short way farther down, bear left at the next intersection, off the Yellow Loop Trail, and follow the path that stays near the water's edge. Stay straight on this path, passing a trail on the left that ends at the pond, a trail on the right, then another on the left. Take the next trail on the left that goes downhill through a low-lying area (just an eighth of a mile west of the open cranberry bog). This path parallels the eastern side of the pond. Stay on it, ignoring a couple of trails to the right.

After you have walked about forty-five minutes from the parking area (about 1.75 mile), the trail passes between two posts. A few feet later the woods open up a bit at the site of an old sand pit, which is now covered with pine seedlings. At the back side of this small opening is a four-way intersection. Go straight through the intersection, and from there onward keep bearing to the right wherever the trail splits to

Standing dead timber provides cover below the water line for bass and other fish. Various birds and waterfowl use it for perches and nesting cavities.

bring you back toward the south end of the pond near the parking lot. About three-quarters of a mile into your return, you will arrive at the cranberry bog, where the sun is quite welcome after so much time in the shaded woods. On my trip I watched a hawk soar high above the maroon-colored cranberry bog.

The main pond lies just over the crest of the hill (on the right, as you face the cranberry bog where you first arrived). Follow the path along to the right and you will soon be back on the trail you started on, where you can retrace your steps back to the parking area.

Total walking time is about an hour and thirty-five minutes, but allow plenty of time because it's easy to get lost on the unmarked trails on your first visit.

Getting There

From Route 3A in Duxbury take Mayflower Street 1.3 miles. The parking lot will be on your right.

From Route 3 south take Exit 11 (Congress Street) and head toward Duxbury. About 100 feet from the exit turn at the first right onto Lincoln Street. Follow Lincoln Street about 0.8 mile and bear left onto Mayflower Street. Follow Mayflower Street 0.3 mile and bear left where the road forks to stay on Mayflower. The parking lot is about .05 mile farther down Mayflower Street on the left.

Bay Farm Conservation Area

Kingston and Duxbury
Approximately 90 acres

Recommended walk: Orange Loop Trail,
$3/4$ mile, 25 minutes

This unique coastal property, located on Kingston Bay, offers nature lovers superb birdwatching. Shore birds, ducks, songbirds, and birds of prey all share fields, woods, and the shore of Bay Farm. An occasional rabbit and red fox are also seen here.

The southern terminus of the Bay Circuit Trail will end at Bay Farm, and I cannot envision a more appropriate finish (or start) to the trailway. After miles of inland hiking Bay Farm, with its beautiful ocean views, will serve as a reward to those who complete a trek on the Bay Circuit.

Bay Farm was once the site of a dairy farm and was purchased by the town of Duxbury in 1972. The adjacent acres in Kingston were also protected from development when the Trust for Public Lands, the Massachusetts Department of Environmental Management, and the town of Kingston jointly purchased the property. It is these kinds of combined efforts that offer our best hope for saving small islands of greenery and open space.

A small rocky perch allows for good migratory- bird viewing on Kingston Bay.

The most impressive feature at Bay Farm is its secluded shoreline along Kingston Bay. It can be easily reached by following the wide, grassy path that leaves the parking area and cuts through the main field, heading directly eastward toward the ocean. The vegetation and wildflowers in the field attract a wide assortment of butterflies and birds. Look for goldfinches with their yellow breasts and black wings and tails. When in flight they often dip like a roller coaster and sing out "per-chiko-ree." The fields also attract northern harriers, which fly a few feet above the ground, tilting from side to side as they scan the meadow for any signs of movement. Duxbury Conservation Commission Administrator Joe Grady says that many different birds of prey are seen here hunting for mice. There have even been sightings of osprey along the shoreline.

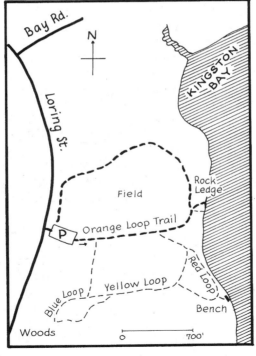

The trail that leads straight through the meadow is the Orange Loop Trail. It makes a loop of the northern end of the property, and it is an excellent trail for children because it is flat, with a length of under a mile. The rock ledges on the bay—a short right off the main trail—are an excellent spot to sit and enjoy the sights, sounds, and smells of the ocean. Look for cormorants diving beneath the water's surface as they hunt for fish. In the winter, another diving bird, the common loon, is sometimes seen here. The loon's underwater feats are legendary, but their flight is equally impressive—surprisingly fast and direct. (Remember that the distinctive summertime black-and-white coloring of the loon is replaced in winter by brownish gray feathers.)

The return walk on the Orange Loop Trail hugs the edge of the field where cedars and a few maples grow. Cedars are opportunistic trees that are among the first species to establish themselves in abandoned fields, and they would quickly take over Bay Farm if not for the annual mowing. This north end of the property is where I often see rabbits, and it would not surprise me if coyotes hunted here at night.

The southern end of the property is also great to explore. There is a bench situated at the shoreline where you can watch the boats crisscross the calm waters of the bay. Look across the water to the northeast and you will see the Myles Standish Monument rising above a little hill. Imagine for a moment how beautiful the South Shore looked when the Pilgrims first arrived. The Pilgrims were surprised to see some coastal land cleared. Wampanoag Native Americans had been farming here, growing corn, beans, and a variety of squashes. But when the Pilgrims landed, there were few Native Americans to be found in the immediate vicinity; most had been killed by disease introduced by the first explorers.

There is a confusing network of short trails at the southern end of Bay Farm, most of which pass through woods of cedar, sumac, and oak. In a small area like this, getting temporarily lost is no big deal, and the woodlands give one the opportunity to see more secretive birds like warblers and the gray catbird.

After exploring Bay Farm you might want to visit Duxbury Beach, one of the longest barrier beaches in Massachusetts and an important stop along the Atlantic coastal flyway. The Powder Point Bridge connects the beach to the mainland, and it is believed to be the longest wooden bridge in the United States. (There is a small parking area adjacent to the Powder Point Bridge just off of Powder Point Avenue at Duxbury's northern end.)

Getting There

To reach Bay Farm take Exit 10 off Route 3 and go northeastward on Route 3A about a half-mile into Duxbury. Go right on Parks Street about half a mile and then bear left on Loring Street. The parking area will be on your left about another half-mile down Loring Street.

Lowell Holly Reservation
Mashpee/Sandwich
135 acres

Recommended walk: 2 miles, 1 hour

Whenever I see shoreline cut off from public access due to private ownership, I soothe my feelings of dismay by thinking of the two miles of shoreline within Lowell Holly Reservation. It's a special place where cool breezes coming off the waters of Wakeby Pond and Mashpee Pond pass over the large stand of massive beech trees that shade this peninsula dividing the two ponds. Small pockets of white, sandy beaches, over 300 native American holly, and several kinds of rhododendrons are just some of the additional reasons to visit the reservation.

Lowell Holly was donated to The Trustees of Reservations in 1934 by Abbott Lawrence Lowell, former president of Harvard College. Except for the cart paths constructed by Dr. Lowell, the reservation has been left primarily in its wild state for the past 200 years. The beech trees are the largest and most impressive I've seen anywhere and quite different than the typical oaks and pines that cover so much of the Cape. Their smooth gray trunks stand out like sentinels guarding the peninsula. In the wintertime the lower branches of the beech often retain their

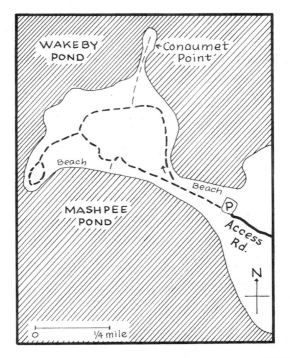

dried yellow-brown leaves, contrasting beautifully against the snow.

Near the parking area is a small sandy beach and picnic tables that are positioned for views of the water. Mashpee and Wakeby ponds are well known for their excellent fishing. Trout are stocked in both the spring and fall. Warm-water species are also present, including largemouth bass, smallmouth bass, pickerel, and bluegill.

A beech tree stands at the sparkling shore of Wakeby Pond at Lowell Holly Reservation.

To begin your walk follow the main path, which hugs the right (north) shoreline. Holly trees are scattered about the understory and thrive quite well in the shade of the beech trees. Any walk through the woods is made more pleasant when you can see deep blue water through the green foilage. The body of water visible through the trees on the right is Wakeby Pond.

One trail winds its way out to narrow Conaumet Point while another goes to the southern tip of the pennisula. It seems many visitors come to enjoy the beach, but few bother to walk out to the end of the peninsula, so chances are you will have the woods to yourself. Be warned, however, that the trails are unmarked and get a bit confusing. (For that reason I don't recommend hiking with children here, but the main beach area near the parking lot is perfect for youngsters.)

The trail to the southern end of the peninsula leads to a sixty-foot-high knoll near the end of the peninsula. Take a moment to climb down to the water's edge where the two ponds are connected by a narrow passage of water. Thoreau knew how to relax at such a spot: "It is soothing employment on one of those fine days in the fall when all the warmth of the sun is fully appreciated, to sit on a stump and overlook the pond."

Imagine how this entire region must have looked before the first Europeans arrived and the Wampanoags roamed all over the Cape hunting and fishing. Surely this peninsula was a favorite camp of theirs. (There is an excellent museum, the Wampanoag Indian Museum, located in Mashpee on Route 130.)

The ponds attract a variety of bird life, including great blue herons, ducks, and Canada geese, and some lucky hikers have spotted osprey. Frequent visitors have told me they occasionally see raccoons and foxes. One such visitor I met had just returned from Alaska and said he has been coming here to ease his transition back to the East Coast because "Lowell

Holly is one of the wildest places on the Cape." He's right—we all need places of peace and solitude close to home.

Walking back toward the parking area, you can follow the trail that hugs the Mashpee-Pond-side of the peninsula. There are some very large holly trees on this side along with more open patches of sandy beaches. In the spring the pink and white flowers of the rhododendron and mountain laurel are especially handsome. Total walking time is about an hour.

Lowell Holly is open from Memorial Day to Columbus Day, 9:00 AM to 5 PM. A ranger is on duty weekends and holidays. Admission is charged. For more information, call 617-821-2977.

Getting There

From Route 6, Exit 2, take Route 130 south 1.4 miles. Go left on Cotuit Road 3.4 miles, then right on South Sandwich Road 0.7 mile to the entrance on the right. Proceed down a narrow dirt road, which will bring you to the parking area.

Ashumet Holly Reservation and Wildlife Sanctuary
East Falmouth
45 acres

Recommended walk: 2 miles, 1 hour

In an effort to protect Cape Cod's native American holly trees, horticulturist Wilfrid Wheeler began this plantation in 1925. When the Massachusetts Audubon Society acquired the property in 1965, there were over 1,000 holly trees on the property, many of which were planted by Wheeler. The trees included at least 65 varieties transplanted from sites all over the northeastern United States. Besides the hollies there were other unusual trees such as a stand of shrublike Franklinia trees that flower in the fall.

This is a small reservation, but the presence of so many holly trees makes it worth the trip. The property is comprised of mixed woodlands and fields that surround a small pond. To start your hike follow the grass-covered path leading away from the parking lot. The trails are color-coded; blue dots mark the path away from the parking area and yellow dots mark the return path. (A detailed map and booklet are available near the main entrance and may be borrowed.)

Red cedars line the trail with taller pitch pines scattered about. After a short distance you will reach

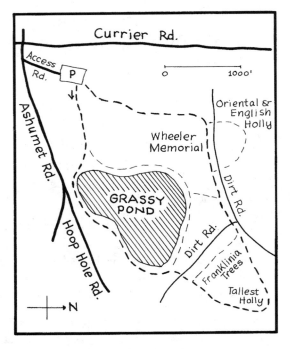

an intersection near Grassy Pond where you should follow the trail to the right. Grassy Pond has an unstable water level, so the plants growing there must be able to survive in this small pond. The water in Grassy Pond is entirely dependent on drainage from nearby hills and the level of water in the ground table—no brook enters or exits the pond. Like most of the ponds on the Cape, Grassy Pond is a kettle hole pond, a remnant of the ice age, formed when huge blocks of ice fell from the glaciers and then melted, forming a kettle-shaped basin.

When you reach the back side of the pond you will see that the holly trees are growing in abundance. Birds are attracted to the trees in autumn and winter, when they eat the berries. Hermit thrush, mocking-

Over sixty-five varieties of holly trees surround the quiet wooded trails of Ashumet Holly Reservation and Wildlife Sanctuary.

birds, cedar waxwings, bobwhites, and ruffed grouse all rely on the fruit as an important food source.

I enjoy walking the perimeter of the property. When you reach the back end of the pond, go straight, crossing a dirt road, rather than bearing left around the pond. The trail heads in a northerly direction and then swings around to the southwest, heading back toward the parking area.

At the northwest end of the pond there is a memorial to Wilfrid Wheeler and a bench positioned perfectly to view the beauty of his labor. A few hemlock and spruce are mixed with the holly and pitch pine, and the various shades of green are soothing to the eye.

To reach the parking area bear left after the Wheeler Memorial. During the spring and summer be on the lookout for barn swallows, which live in the barn by the parking area.

Getting There

From the intersection of Routes 28 and 151 in North Falmouth follow Route 151 for four miles. Turn left on Currier Road. The entrance is 100 yards ahead on the right.

From the Mashpee traffic circle take Route 151 west for three miles. Take a right onto Currier Road. The entrance is 100 yards ahead on the right.

The grounds are open every day except Mondays and major holidays. There is an admission fee.

Bibliography

AMC Massachusetts and Rhode Island Trail Guide. Boston: Appalachian Mountain Club, 1989.

Cahill, Kay. "Programs to glimpse bygone era, fall's splendors." *Boston Globe*, October 1991.

Clayton, Barbara, and Kathleen Whitley. *Exploring Coastal Massachusetts.* New York: Dodd, Mead & Company, 1983.

Fisher, Alan. *Country Walks Near Boston.* Boston: Appalachian Mountain Club, 1986.

Godin, Alfred J. *Wild Mammals of New England.* New York: DeLorme Publishing Company, 1981.

Guide to the Massachusetts Audubon Society's Wildlife Sanctuaries, Nature Centers and Urban Centers. Lincoln, MA: Massachusetts Audubon Society.

Hopkins, Libby O. *A Guide to the Properties of The Trustees of Reservations.* Beverly, MA: The Trustees of Reservations, 1992.

Krutch, Joseph W., ed. *Thoreau: Walden and Other Writings.* New York: Bantam Books, 1962.

Kulik, Stephen et al. *The Audubon Society Field Guide to the Natural Places of the Northeast: Coastal.* New York: Pantheon Books, 1984.

Moose Hill Wildlife Sanctuary Newsletter. Massachusetts Audubon Society, No. 3, 2 (1991).

The Newsletter of Tower Hill Botanic Garden. Boylston, MA: 1992.

Niering, William A. *Wetlands*. New York: Alfred A. Knopf, 1985.

Passport to Essex County Greenbelt. Essex, MA: Essex County Greenbelt Association, 1983.

Perry, John and Jane G. Perry. *The Sierra Club Guide to the Natural Areas of New England*. San Francisco: Sierra Club Books, 1990.

Petrides, George A. *Eastern Trees*. Boston: Houghton Mifflin Company, 1988.

Primack, Mark L. *Greater Boston Park and Recreation Guide*. Chester, CT: Globe Pequot Press, 1983.

Robbins, Chandler S., Herbert Zim, and Bertel Bruun. *Birds of North America*. New York: Golden Press, 1983.

Roth, Charles E. *Black Pond Nature Preserve*. Massachusetts Audubon Society and The Nature Conservancy Booklet.

Roth, Judy. "A Pratt Farm Visit." *Hometown Magazine*, October 1988.

Scheller, William G. *More Country Walks Near Boston*. Boston: Appalachian Mountain Club, 1984.

Siegler, Hilbert R. *Yankee Wildlife*. Orford, NH: Equity Publishing, 1982.

Thoreau, Henry D. *The Natural History Essays*. Salt Lake City: Peregrine Smith Books, 1980.

———.*The River*. New York: Bramhall House, 1963. (Selections from Thoreau's Journal.)

Tougias, Mike. *The Hidden Charles*. Emmaus, PA: Yankee Books, 1991.

Wertz, Raoul. "The Bay Circuit and Trek II." *Appalachia Bulletin*, 1991.

White, Brian and John Brady. *Fifty Hikes in Massachusetts*. Woodstock, VT: Backcountry Publications, 1983.

About the Author

MICHAEL TOUGIAS is a native New Englander who writes on a wide range of topics including history, nature, gardening, and travel. He is the author of *The Hidden Charles* and *Country Roads of Massachusetts*. His articles have appeared in dozens of publications such as the *Boston Glode*, *Fine Gardening*, and *Trout* magazine. He currently writes a monthly travel column for local newspapers about his rambles in Massachusetts.

It took him four years to research and write *Nature Walks in Eastern Massachusetts*. He estimates that he walked over 700 miles and took about the same number of photographs.

In his free time he enjoys hiking with his family, fishing, canoeing, and reading. When not exploring Massachusetts, he spends time at his rustic cabin in northern Vermont.

About the AMC

THE Appalachian Mountain Club is where recreation and conservation meet. More than 64,000 members have joined the AMC to pursue their interests in hiking, canoeing, skiing, walking, rock climbing, bicycling, camping, kayaking, and backpacking, and—at the same time—to help safeguard the environment in which these activities are possible.

Since it was founded in 1876, the Club has been at the forefront of the environmental protection movement. By cofounding several of New England's leading environmental organizations, and working in coalition with these and many more groups, the AMC has influenced legislation and public opinion.

Volunteers in each chapter lead hundreds of outdoor activities and excursions and offer introductory instruction in backcountry sports. The AMC education department offers members and the public a wide range of workshops, from introductory camping to the intensive Mountain Leadership School taught on the trails of the White Mountains.

The most recent efforts in the AMC conservation program include river protection, Northern Forest Lands policy, support for the American Heritage Trust, Sterling Forest (NY) preservation, and support for the Clean Air Act.

The AMC's research department focuses on the forces affecting the ecosystem, including ozone levels, acid rain and fog, climate change, rare flora and habitat protection, and air quality and visibility.

The AMC Volunteer Trails Program is active throughout the AMC's twelve chapters and maintains over 1,200 miles of trails, including 350 miles of the Appalachian Trail. Under the supervision of experienced leaders, hundreds of volunteers spend from one afternoon to two weeks working on trail projects.

At the AMC headquarters in Boston and at Pinkham Notch Visitor Center in New Hampshire, the bookstore and information center stock the entire line of AMC publications, as well as other trail and river guides, maps, reference materials, and the latest articles on conservation issues. Guidebooks and other AMC gifts are available by mail order (AMC, P.O. Box 298, Gorham NH 03581), or call toll-free 800-262-4455. Also available from the bookstore or by subscription is *Appalachia*, the country's oldest mountaineering and conservation journal.

Begin a New Adventure—Join the AMC

We invite you to join the Appalachian Mountain Club and share the benefits of membership. Every member receives *AMC Outdoors*, the membership magazine that, ten times a year, brings you not only news about environmental issues and AMC projects, but also listings of outdoor activities, workshops, excursions, and volunteer opportunities. Members also enjoy discounts on AMC books, maps, educational workshops, and guided hikes, as well as reduced fees at all AMC huts and lodges in Massachusetts and New Hampshire.

To join, send a check for $40 for an adult membership, or $65 for a family membership to AMC, Dept. S7, 5 Joy Street, Boston MA 02108; or call 617-523-0636 for payment by Visa or MasterCard.   S7

Alphabetical Listing of Areas